Sophiatown

Sophiatown

Coming of Age in South Africa

Don Mattera

Beacon Press   Boston

Beacon Press
25 Beacon Street
Boston, Massachusetts 02108

Beacon Press books
are published under the auspices of
the Unitarian Universalist Association of Congregations.

96 95 94 93 92 91 90 89   1 2 3 4 5 6 7 8

Library of Congress Cataloging-in-Publication Data
Mattera, Don, 1935–
Sophiatown : coming of age in South Africa.
British ed. published under title: Gone with the twilight.
1. Mattera, Don, 1935–   . 2. Poets, South
African—20th century—Biography. 3. Journalists—
South Africa—Biography. 4. Sophiatown (Johannesburg,
South Africa)—Biography. 5. Johannesburg (South
Africa)—Biography. 6. Colored people (South Africa)—
Politics and government. 7. South Africa—Race rela-
tions. I. Title.
PR9369.3.M374Z477 1989   821 [B]   88-47885
ISBN 0-8070-0206-2

To My Country and My People –
and their refusal to kneel before guns

Contents

Introduction

Bernard Magubane

Whatever the case, action is a reality! It forms part of that given existence from which the "magical" mind which claims to grasp and arrest the world may well emerge in order to hurl itself into the void but which it can transcend only illusorily. Action is a reality.
                                        —Henry Lafebvre, *Dialectical Materialism*

Don Mattera's autobiographical essay is an example of the kind of action that Lafebvre describes in the passage above. Mattera's poetry and books about the black condition and struggles in South Africa derive not from contemplation but from the thick of struggle. It is the combination of theory and practice that has earned Mattera the title of the bard of the people's liberation struggle. The story of his life in Sophiatown as told in this essay is intricate. Covering Mattera's teenage years from 1948 to 1962 when Sophiatown was bulldozed out of existence, it weaves together both his personal experience and political development.

Through Mattera's personal recollections we come as close as possible to a glimpse of how history actually happens, how one individual achieves self-awareness and moves from self-estrangement to become a conscious actor in history. In telling the story of his life as a "colored" teenager, Mattera takes on the ambitious goal of making us recapture the crucial events of the 1950s in Sophiatown, one of the most important decades in the history of black political struggles in South Africa.

The Nationalist Party, which came to power in 1948 and has ruled South Africa ever since, chose as its main election issue the extension of the policy of apartheid, or *baaskap* (literally "boss rule"), to all areas of life. The election of this party, which espoused naked white supremacy, posed a serious challenge to black people throughout the country. The African National Congress (ANC), which had been founded in 1912, and the South African Indian Congress, formed by Mahatma Gandhi in 1908, worked out an alliance to resist the policies of the Nationalist Party and called on other ethnic parties to join them. The result was the Congress Alliance (CA) made up of the ANC, SAIC, the Coloured People's Organization, and the White Congress of Democrats. In 1952 the CA launched the Defiance Campaign—a nonviolent challenge to the apartheid laws. The aim of apartheid's legal super-structure was to freeze black political expression by imposing a legal framework of unbelievable harshness and cruelty.

It was this atmosphere of ANC-led resistance that played a key role in Mattera's political development and that made him put down the knife and gun (as gang leader) and take up the pen. One of the orga-nizations that Mattera participated in was the Western Areas Student Association, a branch of the ANC's youth wing. He also worked as a journalist and was the founder of the Union of Black Journalists. In 1986 he helped to found the Congress of South African Writers and after the banning of the Black Consciousness Movement became an executive member of the National Forum. These activities resulted in his being placed under house arrest and in his political banning.

Mattera might have remained a leader of the notorious Vultures gang, which he formed and which terrorized the people of Sophiatown in the early 1950s, had the Nationalist Party not embarked on its policy of "cleaning" the so-called black spots in white areas through the Group Areas Act of 1950. The resistance to this Act, which sought to racially segregate residential areas, aroused the political consciousness of large numbers of people, including Mattera. He recalls attending mass meetings held in the Freedom Square of Newclare and Sophiatown, where he heard the ANC leaders Dr. Alfred Xuma, Dr. Y. M. Dadoo, Moses Kotane, O. R. Thambo, Nana Sita, Robert Resha, and others denounce the evils of apartheid. ANC activists like Robert Resha mo-tivated gangs to redirect their frustrations to political activity, and in particular urged them to join the Defiance Campaign. Two individuals in particular made a great impact on Mattera's life: Father Trevor Hud-dleston, an Anglican priest whose parish was in Sophiatown, and Nana Sita, the leader of the South African Indian Congress and Gandhi's follower. Speaking of the latter, Mattera writes: "Few men in this world continue to live beyond their graves; Nana Sita was one of them. He had transformed despair into hope; fear into understanding; cowardice into courage" (p.11).

Sophiatown proved that black and white can live side by side. In this ghetto black intellectuals and whites discussed Shakespeare while en-joying American jazz in the subeens (speakeasies). *Drum Magazine* helped many aspiring black writers of fiction to get started. It was in Sophiatown that African traditional music and Afro-American jazz pro-duced a new synthesis called Tsaba-Tsaba, a musical form that propelled

Miriam Makeba, Hugh Masekela and others to international fame. And yet the die-hard racists, decided that Sophiatown had to be razed to the ground—it produced too many troublesome "natives."

Sophiatown

The Mattera family settled in Sophiatown, a slum near Johannesburg, where Don Mattera was born fifty-three years ago. Johannesburg itself is a product of the larger forces of world imperialism and finance, and especially it is a product of the discovery of gold in 1885–86. Johannesburg's phenomenal growth is described as follows by Charles Van Onslen:

> The mining capitalist revolution that occurred on the Witwatersrand between 1886 and 1914 created and transformed Johannesburg. From a diggers' camp of about 3,000 adventurers in 1887, there developed first a mining town with a population of over 100,000 people in 1896, and then, by 1914, an industrialising city with over a quarter of a million inhabitants. From the tented mining camp at the diggings in the 1880s, there grew the single-quarters and boarding-houses of corrugated-iron that clustered around the deep-level mines and city centre in the 1890s, and then the more substantial brick-built homes of the working class and other suburbs by 1914. This dramatic surge and spread of population also reflected itself in other ways, for example in the changing municipal boundaries of Johannesburg. In 1898 the Town Council held jurisdiction over an area of five square miles; when the nominated Town Council under the occupying British forces first took control in 1901 this was extended to nine square miles; and by the time that civilian local government was firmly reestablished in 1903 this had yet again increased to an enormous 82 square miles.[1]

Sophiatown was spawned by the same forces that brought Johannesburg into being. Originally, Sophiatown was part of a farm called Waterval, which was bought by a white businessman named Tobiansky, who, after leasing it to the government for a few years, decided to build a township in memory of his wife and family after World War I. Some of the streets that form part of Mattera's story were named after Tobiansky's children—Edith, Gerty, Bertha, Toby, Sol. The farm was divided into small building plots or stands—50 by 100 feet, or 50 by 50 feet, bought intially by whites from Tobiansky. But by 1910 the town clerk was reporting that the township owners were selling the plots to anyone who had money. In 1912 a Johannesburg Town Council report observed that "there are in Johannesburg suburbs, some of the stands of which were originally sold to white men, and where natives can now obtain ownership of stands on very reasonable terms. In Sophiatown, for example, we have a mixed population of black and white."[2]

This, then, is the origin of the racial mixture of the population of Sophiatown. When the city built a sewage-disposal system next to Sophiatown at the end of World War I, many whites left the town and moved to other suburbs such as Krededrop, Brixton, and Mayfair. By the 1940s Sophiatown had become a demographic quilt—an amalgam of ethnic, social, and cultural groups; a cosmopolitan center of intellectuals, radical politics, jazz, and gangsters.

Mattera describes with sympathy, and even with passion, the life and plight of Sophiatown in the 1950s, when the apartheid regime of the Nationalist Party that had gained power in 1948 decided that the "mixing" of the races and private ownership of the land by blacks contradicted its fundamental tenets and passed the Group Areas Act, which would set aside racially segregated residential areas for each ethnic group.

Many social scientists, including social historians, have observed how racial oppression and domination and the policy of apartheid have fragmented the black population into ethnic and linguistic categories in order to weaken its bonds of community. But these studies have lacked the factuality, the first-hand experience, and the insights that Mattera brings to his subject. Few white social scientists can put themselves in Mattera's shoes or understand fully the tragedy of being of "mixed" parentage under apartheid.

Although life was harsh for Mattera and the people of Sophiatown, it was also full of the creative spirit and constant excitement. Mattera describes with verve Sophiatown's cultural and religious ambiance. The proliferation of fundamentalist sects, for example, indicated not only the harshness of life but the extent of alienation felt by the inhabitants. As Mattera puts it,

The Face of Religion beamed like colourful fluorescent advertisements from the countless Christian sects and Hindu, Moslem and Buddhist segments that preached and sold their understanding of penitence, redemption and reconciliation with God. There were the rituals of the African *amaZioni* with their frenzied worshipping through cymbals and drums that rose and fell from midnight hour until dawn. Men, women, old and young and children called frantically upon their God as if He was on a long, long holiday. Churches competed for the redemption of souls; trying as it were to sell God at a bargain price to people who had stopped buying, not because they had no money, but because they had no faith. . . .

And salvation was going for a song but men, it appeared were not buying. Only older people opened their ears to listen to the song as they gave the remnants of their wasted and broken lives in the final compensatory service to the Great One . . . who ruled the earth and skies. (pp. 75–76)

Sophiatown was a world of brutality, of want, crime, love, beauty, and community. It was a metropolitan melting pot. Mattera has set his experiences and tribulations in the context of the times—the time of great political agitation among the oppressed led by the African National Congress and its allies, the South African Indian Congress, the Communist Party of South Africa (before it was banned in 1950), and the Coloured People's Organization.

The Politics of Being "Coloured"

The reality of being a "coloured" in South Africa underlies the story of Don Mattera's life and the destruction of Sophiatown. Mattera's genealogy runs the gamut of ethnic experience: his paternal grandfather, Franscesco Mattera, was an Italian sailor who married a Griqua woman; Mattera's mother belongs to the Tswana ethnic group. The Griquas themselves are the product of the frontier miscegenation between Boer settlers (descendants of the Dutch) and the Khoikhon (the so-called Hottentots, who are the indigenous inhabitants of the Cape). Mattera is thus well qualified to interpret the implications of color consciousness and racial discrimination in South Africa. He depicts with great clarity and justified anger the indignities that the racial purists of apartheid have inflicted on the African people, who are the majority, but also on the offspring of Europeans—especially the Afrikaners—and Africans.

"Coloured" is a grab-bag category, meaning simply that one is a particular hue, the result of belonging to one of the ethnic groups (or a mixture thereof) that make up the population of South Africa: Africans, Malay slaves, Indians (brought to South Africa as indentured laborers), and whites. South Africa's laws distinguish several groups of coloureds: the Cape coloureds, who are the descendants of the so-called Bushmen

and Hottentots (more accurately known as the Khoisan); the Cape Malay, the original Malay slaves, most of whom did not bring women
with them, and who were brought to South Africa by the Dutch East
India Company settlers; the less well-known coloured "tribe" of the
Maasbieker, "a type of Mozambique coloured"; and the "busters" or
Bastards—half-breeds mainly found in Namibia (South West Africa)
and in parts of the Northern Cape. A fifth group comprises the Mauritian
coloureds, most of them light-skinned and long haired, and who are
chiefly based in Natal. Unlike the Transvaal and the Cape coloureds,
who speak Afrikaans, the Natal coloureds speak English. The most
obnoxious and hated label is "Other Coloureds," which refers to the
offspring of relationships outside the white group, such as the children
of African and Chinese, African and Indian, and Africans and all the
coloured groups listed above. Mattera notes ironically, that "what the
segregationist could not escape was that many of these Bushman and
Hottentot offspring had blue, grey or green eyes with straight blond
hair" (p. 22). However, to be coloured or a person of "mixed-blood"
in terms of the apartheid laws is a double negative: one is both a nonwhite
and a nonblack African.

The attempt to constitute the "coloured" as an ethnic community
separate from black and white has a long history in South Africa in
politics. In the space available here, I can do no more than give a few
examples of the political meaning of being coloured. The constitution
of "coloured" as an ethnic group, by definition, implies an intentional
effort to break the bonds of community between black Africans and
their coloured offspring. This policy was instituted by British colonial
officials just prior to the formation of the Union of South Africa as a
white dominion within the British empire in 1909. The Immorality Act
(which goes back to 1927) and its various amendments—the Population
Registration Act (and its various amendments) and the Group Areas
Act (as amended)—exemplify the legal aspects of this effort and have
made the life of coloureds difficult indeed.

Lord Selborne, high commissioner for South Africa and governor of
the Transvaal and Orange River colonies from 1905 to 1910, spelled
out his policy of making the coloureds a buffer between black and white
in a memo to General Smuts:

> Our object should be to teach the Coloured people to give their loyal
> support to the white population. It seems to me sheer folly to classify

them with Natives, and by treating them as Natives to force them away from their natural allegiance to the whites and into making common cause with the Natives. If they are so forced, in the time of trouble they will furnish exactly those leaders which the Natives could not furnish for themselves. It is, therefore, in my opinion, unwise to think of treating them as Natives; and it would be as unjust as unwise. There are many Coloured people who are quite white inside, though they may be coloured outside. There are some, indeed, who are quite white outside also. The problem of the treatment of the Coloured people is, indeed, sadly complicated by the fact that they vary in every shade of character and colour from pure white inside and outside to pure black inside and outside.

I suggest that the wise policy is to give them the benefit of their white blood—not to lay the stress on the black blood, but to lay the stress on the white blood, and to make any differentiation of treatment between them and whites the exception and not the rule. A case for such differentiation would only arise when a Coloured man showed by his manner of living, e.g., by the practice of polygamy, that he had reverted to the tribal type.[3]

These recommendations are not only wicked; they also reveal an underlying fact about colonialism and its accompanying policy of white supremacy: it is not the head of the colonizer that begins to rot first—it is the heart. Lord Selborne's policy recommendations for the treatment of the Africans are just as sinister:

The objects which the Government must have in their Native policy are: (i) to preserve the peace of the country, for nothing is so demoralizing or injurious to its true welfare as a native war; (ii) to ensure the gradual destruction of the tribal civilization among the Natives; (iii) to ensure the gradual destruction of the tribal system, which is incompatible with civilization. An important feature of this policy will be teaching the Natives to work. A large proportion of them do work now, but mostly in a desultory and inefficient manner. The object must be to teach them to work as continually and effectively as the whites are supposed to but do not always do.[4]

In 1927, as I have said, the first so-called Immorality Act prohibiting sex acts between Europeans and Africans was passed. This Act was rewritten in 1950 by the Nationalist Government and made more specific: it prohibits illicit casual intercourse between whites and nonwhites, and in 1957 its provisions were tightened even further by the Immorality Amendment Act. In 1950 the Population Registration Amendment Act made descent the main factor in determining race classification. Introducing the bill, the minister of the interior said that the new law was necessary because, in spite of previous legislation, there had been "gradual, but nevertheless to my mind dangerous, integration of whites and nonwhites."[5]

The proximity in which poor whites and blacks lived in Sophiatown was one reason why the apartheid government had to destroy it. Indeed, the Population Registration, Mattera rightly explains, "sought to obliterate from [the Boers'] shady genealogical history any genetic connection between themselves and Coloureds" (p. 6).

What the Population Registration Act wanted to achieve genealogically, the Group Areas Act (1950) sought to achieve geographically: it set aside separate residential areas for all ethnic populations. The Group Areas Act of 1950 (as amended in 1966) states that:

> 2. (I) For the purposes of this Act, there shall be the following groups:
> (a) A white group [whose diagnostic characteristics are then stated].
> (b) A native group [whose diagnostic characteristics are then stated].
> (c) A coloured group, in which shall be included:
> (i) Any person who is not a member of the white group or of the native group; and
> (ii) Any woman, to whichever race, tribe, or class she may belong, between whom and a person who is, in terms of sub-paragraph (i), a member of the coloured group, there exists a marriage, or who cohabits with such a person;
> (iii) Any white man between whom and a woman who in terms of sub-paragraph (i) is a member of the coloured group, there exists a marriage, or who cohabits with such a woman.[6]

After 1948 apartheid went much further in its demarcation and classification of people than the previous policy of segregation. In addition to the laws directed at facilitating the exploitation of Africans, laws were enacted that constrained sexual activity of whites, reminding them that the privileges they enjoyed were based on their being conscious of their whiteness. The penalty for committing an "Immoral Act" could be as severe as a seven-year prison term. Thus, in terms of South Africa's race laws, Don Mattera was the product of an "immoral act." What a burden for a child to bear!

Mattera recalls the trauma he experienced when he first went before the Classification Board, which would decide what group he would belong to, "a hotnot or an Italian":

> There had been . . . no blood tests, no scrutiny. I was the Italian's son, and the last-born of the family. If the Boers believed I was my grandpa's son, I was not going to be the one to shatter that belief. My number was 331-591697C; the 'C' stood for coloured but the birth certificate read 'mixed' in the column denoting race. It was the first I knew of a race called mixed. Mixed, though, was far far better than native, and being called kaffir, as many reclassified coloureds were to discover. Heart-rending stories, filled with biting humiliation and anguish, daily made newspaper headlines in the late fifties. Some victims of the reclassification trauma chose suicide to bail them out of their absurd misery. Whole and stable families were shattered overnight as brothers, sisters, sons and daughters were ripped apart by the cruel laws of race separation. Relentless pass raids netted in hundreds of 'borderline' cases; those bordering between African and coloured, not between white and coloured. The latter species would be dealt with only later as the 'other coloured' grouping. (pp. 25–26)

Mattera, even though he is "coloured" by government definition, refused to be called by this cultureless, enigmatic term. He defines himself as a black South African. His falling in love with Dumazile, a Zulu woman, is interesting in the light of his future political identification. It probably was at the time an unconscious rejection of the social and political status that the white minority had assigned to coloureds. Although he could understand why some coloureds, especially the dark-skinned ones, spoke derogatorily about "kaffirs" and "coolies," this attitude was an affront to the values, norms, and very essence of his existence as a product of a cosmopolitan lifestyle and code of conduct: "People were afraid to speak African languages or tune their radios to black stations. Association would mean a common identity with all the humiliation, debasement and suffering that Africans experienced" (p. 149). Even though this attitude was understandable, it nevertheless evoked anger in Mattera. It was tantamount to accepting the white definition of "coloured," an insult in itself.

Violence

The colonialism and the doctrine of white supremacy are based on violence, race hatred, and immoral relations. As Mattera notes, they result in "a battle where white might was right and black lives expendable" (p. 94). Mattera dramatizes and emphasizes the extreme state of alienation that manifests itself in violence.

Growing up in Sophiatown, where bloodshed and violence were common, Don Mattera inevitably became a gangster. Mattera recalls many details of the hideous butcheries he witnessed, not because he takes a morbid delight in them, but because he is thus able to show how this violence among the victims of oppression is a symptom of an extreme self-hatred and alienation, which, once the oppressed develop their political consciousness, can be transformed into constructive political action.

The roots of violence in South Africa are deep. In his book, *The Wretched of the Earth,* Franz Fanon discusses the role of violence in a colonial situation. For Fanon, violence involves somatic injury to human beings, the most radical manifestation of which is the killing of the individual. Thus, Fanon's statement that "colonialism . . . is violence in its natural state," can be applied to places like South Africa, where white minority rule was inaugurated, and is still maintained, by the use of physical violence. To "pacify" the colonized peoples and to compel them to accept the new alien order, the white minority often finds it necessary to wage constant war against them.

Mattera tells us that it is necessary to create a philosophically devalued *Other* in order to maintain a colonial situation in which the destruction of black life is considered a necessary price for white privilege and civilization. In this episode in Mattera's autobiography, shortly before the destruction of Sophiatown, Mattera captures the essence of being the *Other:*

I tugged the Boer's coatsleeve. *'Meneer,* when are you people going to break down our houses? I heard you tell Abram about it.'

I may have been too abrupt, because he jerked his arm away and snarled, 'What the hell do you mean by "you people?" Who is your "you people" . . . eh?'

The Boer's face reddened for a second time. It was not the earlier shame Abram's words had caused him to feel. It was anger at being made the equivalent of a black person. The phrase 'you people' (*'julle mense'*) was and still is for the exclusive use and reserve of the Boers; a term through which they separate themselves from the rest of the indigenous folk of Southern Africa. *'Ons mense'* (our people)—which is a term of endearment to them, is diametrically opposed to *'julle mense'* whenever political, educational, social and religious lines have to be defined. Say *'julle mense'* to a group of diehard Afrikaner nationalists and you could end up lying on your back (p. 8).

Between blacks and the white rulers of South Africa, there can be no genuinely human contact; only relations of domination, forced labor, intimidation by the police and army, submission, and contempt as exemplified by "Baas Pottie." When the "native" becomes cheeky there is always force lurking in the background. As Mattera puts it:

> I tell you I have heard and read of the strength of collective resolve, but I have seen the firepower of this regime shatter angry and determined men, rich and poor alike. In the white man's court or on the battlefronts of the streets, firepower always won. For the law that spoke in the court was the same law that blasted in the street. The white man and the law were indivisible. . . . (p. 9).

Evil, we know, is necessary for good to exist, matter for idea, and darkness for light. In South Africa the artificial creation of blacks as evil *Other*, the defiler of white civilization, is inevitable.

There are several conclusions that can be drawn from this creation of the *Other*. First, the *Other* is always seen in negative terms, as a lack, a void, as deficient in human qualities, whatever those qualities may be. Mattera sees the structural violence of white minority rule in South Africa as a kind of manichaeism that includes "the power to destroy and the pain of being destroyed . . . dust" (p. 18). Furthermore, the *Other* becomes "opaque." "In this country you are what they think you should be, what they want you to be, and all that through the stroke of a pen" (p. 23). To be constituted as the *Other* inflicts another form of violence—psychological violence, which is, in Galtung's words, "violence that works on the soul."[7]

The physical squalor of Sophiatown and other towns is also part of the process of dehumanizing the black population. The heterogeneity and randomness of Sophiatown, in the words of Raymond Williams, "embodied a system: a negative system of indifference; a positive system of differentiation, a law, a power, financial control."[8] And those responsible for this evil, according to Mattera, are the white voters of South Africa and their government (p. 10).

The genius and originality of Mattera's autobiography lie in his ability to dramatize those social actors and the consequences of their immoral actions that are normally ignored when we talk about apartheid. Mattera's autobiographical method is remarkable. Sophiatown is shown as at once a social fact and a human landscape. Mattera conducts us into the buses and streets of Sophiatown, and through his life we can experience these mean streets.

Conclusion

Sophiatown is a book created from careful and knowing memory and observations; from the first-hand experience of gang life; from the recollections of the mood in Sophiatown in the 1950s, especially the political opposition to the Group Areas Act that was passed by the Nationalist regime to destroy communities like Sophiatown. All these events are written in a prose that, Mattera says, may not be pristine English but is keen enough to draw blood and tears.

In Mattera's Sophiatown, the real relationships of human beings to each other, their social motives which, unknown even to the actors, govern their actions, thoughts, and emotions, are revealed with great candor and honesty. Mattera's political evolution to black consciousness reveals an increasing loathing of the white oppressor and the system of apartheid created to exploit and degrade black labor.

Mattera's evolution from a gangster to a poet for the black consciousness movement is one of the great stories of human potential, a story similar to that of Malcolm X in the United States. Mattera's tough tale is an extraordinary sign of the times; it tells us that the poor and downtrodden in South Africa want their freedom, as the ANC slogan of the 1950s put it, "in their lifetime." The manner in which Mattera tells his story, against the background of the larger struggles that were going on in the 1950s, will ensure its place as one of the historic documents of our era.

It is ironic that, thirty years after Sophiatown was destroyed, Mattera has succeeded in making us appreciate what an important period it was in the struggle for liberation; indeed, he makes clear that all the forces that are active today in South Africa had their origin in the 1950s.

"Memory is a weapon," he tells us, "I know deep down inside of me, in that place where laws and guns cannot reach nor jackboots trample, that there had been no defeat. In another day, another time, we would emerge to reclaim our dignity and our land. It was only a matter of time and Sophiatown would be reborn" (p. 151).

As the resistance moves from protest to struggle, Mattera's book should help not only to mobilize the masses, but to deepen their awareness that they are standing on the shoulders of giants: Mandela, Sisilu, Mbeki, Slovo, Kathadra, and many others who helped shape Mattera's political consciousness. His poem "Heat of Chains" sums up the current situation in South Africa:

What dreams and visions we have clutched
In our frantic search for life
Are singed by the heat of our chains
Nothing remains
But anger,
At ourselves and God
Reconciliation and amity
Drown in a whirlpool of unrelenting dogma
What hope existed for a bloodless revolt
Now lies shattered into a million fragments of
    despair
There is no bloodless war and there can never
    be asylum for expediency
What the soldiers have taken from us
    we must reclaim
And if we must weep
Oh, let us weep gently,
Committing our pain
To our cause
And with one blow
Silence these fiends
Who laugh as we die . . .

Notes

1. Charles Van Onslen, *Studies in the Social and Economic History of the Witwatersrand* (Johannesburg: Ravan Press, 1982), 163.

2. Quoted in Luli Callinicos, *Working Life, Factories, Townships and Popular Culture on the Rand, 1896–1940* (Johannesburg: Ravan Press, 1987), 2:179–80.

3. Quoted in J. C. Smith, *Selections from the Smuts Papers,* ed. W. K. Hancock and Jean Van Der Poel (Cambridge: Cambridge University Press, 1966), 2:337.

4. Ibid.

5. Brian Bunting, *The Rise of the South African Rich* (Baltimore: Penguin Books, 1969), 189.

6. Quoted in John Western, *Outcast Cape Town* (Minneapolis: University of Minnesota Press, 1981), 9.

7. John Galtung, "Violence, Peace and Peace Research," *Journal of Peace Research* 3 (1969):169.

8. Raymond Williams, *The Country and City* (London: Oxford University Press, 1973), 154.

1. Demolition

Wednesday 22 July 1962. The night had been a restless one, nightmarish and foreboding. I awoke in a cold sweat. The room was stuffy and I was choking. Fresh air, God how I needed fresh air to rush into my lungs and fill them with a burst of life. I opened the squeaking door and the crisp, sharp breath of the early morning pricked my nostrils. I drew in great gasps of the life-giving gas. Refreshed in mind but not in body, I noticed with a slight irritation that the dirt bin had been toppled over by the township's ever-hungry dogs. Scraps of debris blew against my legs when a sudden cold breeze whipped the untied gate. The dusty, untarred street, once crushed and trampled on by thousands of black feet, was subdued and uninhabited. The sound of motor vehicles revving incessantly burst the stillness.

Life came to the streets in the age-old tradition; silhouettes of moving objects and people who spoke in hushed and muffled tones. The winter had been unkind and the two-room council shacks permeated that unkindness into our very beds. The thin chimneys gave out smoke-signals. Just looking at the smoke itself gave one hope. Only a few homes had electric power and the majority of the residents of Western Native Township used coal stoves and paraffin appliances for cooking, lighting and heating.

Many people lived and died by candlelight.

As a child I had always loved and been deeply fascinated by the outlines of trees and the silhouette movement of people at dusk, and at those pristine hours preceding dawn. The magical sound of voices fading in the distance, of workers on their way to the city, or the sight of the crouched or straight figures of women carrying the usual bundles on their heads — washed and neatly pressed for the madams of white Johannesburg. These moments brought with them the sense of proximity and warmth I had enjoyed when my mother was employed at the homes of white people. I used to marvel at the grace and ease with which black women balanced the huge bundles on their heads, jabbering away at each other as if they didn't have a care in the world.

Wrinkled grandmamas or middle-aged aunts, these women were mobile laundry services, domestic workers, child governesses, cooks and 'errand girls' all wrapped in one. My mother was one of them and she spent all her adolescence and adult life giving to the children of her employers those things that I should have received. For many black women these jobs were, and still are, a source of vital income; some of these women were, and still are, sole breadwinners. Work was work; besides there were kind and thoughtful employers.

I was unemployed at the time and penniless. What money I had was spent on food and clothes for my young children: Anthony who was five at the time, and Teressa, a two-year-old. My common-law wife Martha, who was expecting our third child, was fast asleep. Ethnically, she was a Shangaan. Her forefathers had travelled from Mozambique into the Northern Transvaal in South Africa, and finally settled in Sophiatown, Johannesburg.

I had met her on my release from prison in February of 1956 after I was acquitted on a murder charge. Martha was sitting on a wooden bench at the bus terminus on the corner of Millar and Victoria

Streets in Sophiatown. A coal brazier burned hot and red in front of her. Yellow maize cobs crackled and braised in the heat. Near her was a huge tin which contained several cooked and steaming cobs. Pearly-white teeth shone in her mouth and her eyes were as big as two full moons. A few minutes later she was mine, like so many other girls in Sophiatown and Western Native Township. During those days it was risky business to refuse me, the leader of the Vultures gang. It didn't matter whether a girl loved me or not; it was one of the fringe benefits of being a gangster.

I left the yard plagued by bad thoughts. A man on a bicycle cursed, swore and kicked at the dogs that barked and snapped at his heels. I found a stone and flung it wildly at them, hitting one so that it yelped. The barking stopped and the man continued his journey in peace. Behind him in the east, the sun appeared to be rising from the concrete cradle of the Golden City, Johannesburg. The first weak rays kissed the shacks dispassionately, almost shyly like a girl on her first date. Abram's Supply Store in Gerty Street, the Sophiatown street where my folks lived before the removals had, as well as the familiar smell of groceries, many bitter-sweet memories. Errands that I ran for my family and our neighbours, the fights and games I shared with other kids, all came alive as I moved around the shop.

Abram, a tall Indian trader with a hooked nose and beady, alert eyes, was well-known to me and my family. I remember him best as the man who had paid young urchins, including me, a pittance for selling vegetables from early morning to sunset. A shrewd and capable businessman, Abram always sold his goods cheaper than the other shops. If you had something to sell and needed quick money, Abram would buy. He was loved by the worst thieves in the business because he never squealed on anyone when the going got tough. I knew many white inspectors who 'ate' from his hands. As an African saying goes: 'When a man is eating, his eyes hardly stray'. Essop, Abram's eldest son, was one of my closest friends; in fact we took care of each other: I protected him with my fists, and he reciprocated with his father's money or goods. Some cynical people called it protection fees, but I saw his response as an act of mutual understanding. I was no Al Capone.

Abram was chewing on that red stuff commonly eaten by some Indians. He kept nodding as someone hidden from my view spoke to him.

'*Ja*, Mattera was very, very lucky. Do you know what he got for his stands? Almost nine thousand pounds. Nine thousand! You tell me a rich man like him still getting all that money!' The speaker moved briefly into my line of vision. He was a huge Boer called Potgieter whose big eyes sat in a coarse and heavily wrinkled face with unusually large, protruding ears. A thick nose jutted out of his face, and although his features gave no indication of this, '*Baas* Pottie' as he preferred to be called, was a kind soul. His tobacco-stained teeth hardly moved as he addressed the Indian trader. The discussion continued: '*Ja jong*, old Mattera was blerry lucky.' This time there was a note of envy in Potgieter's voice. 'Even that native doctor, *ou* Xuma, for all his communist politics, didn't get half as much, and he's one of those Congress people who went to court about refusing to move. Do you remember all those threats? Xuma has gone and we now know who the *real* bosses are.' His eyes glowed and some powerful oxygen filled his lungs so that his chest expanded to twice its normal size.

I knew then that pride was the child of victory. . . .

Abram nodded sheepishly. But he knew in his heart of hearts that someday he too would be forced to pack up and sell; it was just a matter of time. The reddish juice rolled from the side of his mouth as he spoke. 'I've often wondered what that old Italian did with his money,' said Abram, and then answering himself, he added, 'Those good-for-nothing sons of his must have wasted most of it on liquor and women. If there's one family that should have ended up being millionaires it's those Matteras. But what can you expect from coloured people?' My blood boiled.

'Ah huh,' agreed the Boer without further ado. What the Indian had said about the liquor and the women was true; it was his generalisation about coloureds that needled me.

'You know *meneer*,' said Abram, using the Afrikaans word for mister, 'I remember when Mattera still had buses and lots of money; I can't understand what happened to that family. They must be cursed or something.'

His words cut deep and though they were a bitter indictment, they were true because my grandfather's children, with few exceptions, had wasted their lives on drink, mostly the destructive concoctions brewed in the township shebeens. The bus company had had to be sold because of the irresponsibility of my uncles. When I looked at

Potgieter and saw the unctuous expression in his face, I understood why he had so readily concurred with the Indian's generalisation about coloureds.

Abram said, 'So *meneer*, you say Mattera's houses are coming down tomorrow, eh?'

'*Ja*,' came the cold reply. 'But it wasn't really necessary for him to move out, he's a white man and the law doesn't really apply to him. We told him so but he chose to move to Albertsville to be close to his daughter. The irony is that Albertsville has also been allocated to whites, but knowing him, I'm sure he will move out again to live with his coloured family.'

Abram interjected: 'For a white person that Italian is really attached and dedicated to his children. It's not every day that you come across a white man who doesn't dump his coloured offspring; Mattera is a rare case.'

The Indian's face assumed a new and strong bearing, and his words gave me some warmth. I had also been quietly impressed by his perception especially as he had always appeared to be entirely engrossed in his money-spinning wholesale grocery business. Abram was among the wealthiest shopkeepers in Sophiatown and he had a clientele which stretched into areas far beyond the borders of our township. Potgieter nodded sullenly and bit his lower lip. He looked the Indian straight in the eye and frowned, exposing a sea of wrinkles that I had not detected on his face before.

But Abram had also been a victim of subtle extortion perpetrated by members of the police force and government officials like Potgieter who took free supplies of groceries and cigarettes as if they were in silent partnership with him. It was not uncommon to see a burly policeman or some white government official or health inspector enter the store, go behind the counter and help himself to anything he wanted.

. . .How strong are those who wield power and represent the law of the land which is not necessarily the law of justice nor the law of the statute book? How mighty are the men who wear the uniforms of that power and authority, and strut the streets and enter at will, the homes of the unarmed and the fearful.

Abram understood and complied with these displays of power and authority without any visible opposition although his two eldest sons Essop and Ali openly objected to the 'legal' extortion. But their father knew the risks involved in challenging that power and authority. So whenever officialdom strutted arrogantly into his small but well-stocked shop and helped itself to his commodities, all he did was grin fawningly and beguilingly, and greet the leeching Boers.

'Take one, *meneer*; take one you power-mongering man. Take one hundred; one thousand, take all and be damned. . . .'

And the Boers took; for mighty are they who carry guns.

All the Indian and other black people could do was grin and smile while their honour and dignity were trampled on and abused.

When Potgieter looked wryly at the Indian because he had alluded to the paternal loyalty of my grandfather to his family, it was because Abram had obviously touched on a sensitive and sacred subject which was and still is taboo among the Afrikaners. The Boers had sought to obliterate from their shady genealogical history any genetic connection between themselves and the coloureds. The Boer scientists and sociologists and their many blood specialists compiled studies and findings in order to dispel the fears of their own doubting Thomases and refute beyond all reasonable and religious doubt any link with the '*Boesmans* and *Hotnots*' — the derogatory names they gave to the coloureds. Coloureds are a nation unto themselves, assert the Boer geneticists. A nation with its own culture, its own civilisation and its own destiny — a doctrine many coloureds believe and perpetuate in their homes and schools and churches, and in every walk of their lives. A colouredness bloated by a false sense of nationhood; almost white but not black, not African despite the genetic throwbacks. Many of them, supporting the racial theories of the Boers, formed coloureds-only political parties and openly campaigned for nationhood under the apartheid policy.

But despite the purist Boer theses and refutations, there are thousands of African women like my own mother, who know differently. Women who have lived in the backyard rooms and worked in white homes and who, perhaps out of loneliness and a longing for love and physical contact or out of human weakness overcome by the voracious carnality of white men, shared beds with their bosses. These, and other women of darker hues, would have testified against the Boer purists, had it not been for the government's 'Immorality' laws which outlawed sex and marriage across the colour lines.

Women who knew differently, but remained silent for fear of being raided and charged and dragged before the courts to be publicly tried, humiliated and jailed. No. Such secrets are better hidden in the closets of the heart where no policemen or spies can reach, where there are no keyholes to peep through nor trees from which to watch and condemn.

Potgieter appeared to be shaken by Abram's words.

'*Meneer,*' the Indian's voice was somewhat subdued, almost a solicitation. 'Couldn't his houses have been resold?'

The reply was curt and abrupt: 'No, they are too old; unlike those of Dr Xuma or Nanabhay in Toby Street which have already been bought. There was no need for Mattera to have moved out; he's a white man you know.' Potgieter's words were empty, directed to himself; tokens of unspoken remorse and contrition.

'*He's a white man*. . . .' What did it matter that a man was white? Did black men not die or feel or bleed when they witnessed the execution of their dignity and manhood? Did black children not stare wide-eyed and afraid when the bulldozers came to their dreams like locusts to the corn? Some people cry when they are hurt, others want to kill. That was how I felt.

'The houses will be demolished tomorrow along with those of Marshall and Mafethe the estate agent who initially also gave us some problems over the sale of his other properties.'

The scruffy Afrikaner's words stung me with an intensity I could not understand. I stood momentarily immobilised, my body temperature changed several times. God, what was he saying, and why was I so upset especially as my people had moved out of the houses about six months ago? Was this perhaps the reason for all those dreams about lice and worms crawling out of my body? What horrible dreams they had been. And now was this it? What did this bloody Boer mean: 'will be demolished tomorrow'?

The casual sentence touched a sore and vital spot inside of me. The houses had helped to shape my dreams and had given warmth to my spirit in the company and fellowship of my kin. I moved towards the two men, one a shrewd, scheming businessman and the other an Afrikaner with a soft heart whose mission to uphold and promote Hendrik Verwoerd's apartheid had been tempered with a strange humaneness found only among the early pioneers of his nation. Abram noticed me and suddenly shrugged as if to convey some message to me, the contents of which I already knew.

I tugged the Boer's coatsleeve. *'Meneer,* when are you people going to break down our houses? I heard you tell Abram about it.'

I may have been too abrupt, because he jerked his arm away and snarled, 'what the hell do you mean by "you people"? Who is your "you people". . . eh?'

The Boer's face reddened for a second time. It was not the earlier shame Abram's words had caused him to feel. It was anger at being made the equivalent of a black person. The phrase 'you people' (*'julle mense'*) was and still is for the exclusive use and reserve of the Boers; a term through which they separate themselves from the rest of the indigenous folk of Southern Africa. *'Ons mense'* (our people) — which is a term of endearment to them, is diametrically opposed to *'julle mense'* whenever political, educational, social and religious lines have to be defined. Say *'julle mense'* to a group of diehard Afrikaner nationalists and you could end up lying on your back.

The year was 1962. There were many diehards around then. . . .

Potgieter realised who I was. *'Kleinbooi,'* (Little boy) he said with sudden tenderness, *'Baas* Pottie doesn't go around smashing people's houses — that's for Speedy Demolishers; it's their job although the government pays them. *'Ons wil nie ons hande vuil maak nie; dis hulle werk. . . .'* (We don't want to dirty our hands; it's their job.) So don't 'you people' me, understand! Otherwise *Baas* Pottie can become very nasty, you hear?' Tenderness was now mixed with anger. No wrong moves, I warned myself.

He spoke again. 'Anyway *seun* (son), if it means so much to you, your *oupa's* (grandpa's) houses are coming down tomorrow. Don't ask me the time because I don't think it's going to make any difference to the old man, unless 'you people' have buckets of money hidden somewhere under his big house.'

Abram laughed. Perhaps he believed in the hidden money because lots of people including some of our own relatives were convinced that my grandfather had hidden a bucket of old gold coins in a cellar under his bedroom. All that would be painfully known tomorrow if what the Boer had said was true. As I said earlier, I really liked Potgieter. He had first visited my grandpa as a government official but later frequented our place as a 'friend'. He drank our wine and ate Italian dishes. Sometimes a few pounds nestled quietly in the palm of his hand as a token of our family's gratitude for turning a blind eye to our property so that our black workers might escape the nightly police raids that became a way of life before and after the forced removals to the Meadowlands and Diepkloof group areas. Wine, food and money were a small price, and the old man paid willingly.

As I left the shop I heard Abram call out to me, but I wasn't listening. The coins I had come to buy bread and milk with were moist with the sweat of my hand, and an excitement I could hardly explain overwhelmed me. Why? Why had it suddenly become a matter of such urgency, especially when all my family had already been relocated and scattered to the four winds with not a murmur from any of them? Why this sudden rage that welled up inside of me? God, somebody had to be told. Dammit they should be feeling as I felt. For were pain and sorrow not feelings to be shared among kith and kin? Had our homes not been extraordinary symbols of a way of life in Sophiatown? The questions burned in my mind. I was too disturbed to accept the fact that other, more beautiful and almost palatial houses had been and were daily being crushed and razed to the ground in the name of the white people, through the power of their god, apartheid. . . . This was the law. My grandfather was white according to the statute books and he had been paid a far higher price for his houses than most of the African, Indian and coloured property owners. The orders to these others were strict: sell and move or else. . . . Many rich standowners refused to sell in the hope that they might bargain for better prices. But the removals became commonplace; in numerous instances they were military operations.

. . . I tell you I have heard and read of the strength of collective resolve, but I have seen the firepower of this regime shatter angry and determined men, rich and poor alike. In the white man's court or on the battlefronts of the streets, firepower always won. For the law that spoke in the court was the same law that blasted in the street. The white man and the law were indivisible. . . .

An occasional Indian or African family won some stay of execution in the courts, but finally they too were forced out. Sophiatown, Vrededorp (Fietas to the people), Newclare, Western Native Township, Malay Camp, Albertsville and Alexandra Township were obstacles in the path of apartheid. Go they must. . . this was the law — Verwoerd's dream backed by the army and the police. Moving one group of people out of their homes to accommodate another often sparked racial hostilities and animosity. In the Transvaal, the Africans were the worst victims of the practice so that in some instances relations between them and the coloureds — who came and occupied their homes — were strained.

The real evil-doers — the white voters of South Africa and their government — were almost forgotten as black people who formerly lived as one community now growled angrily at one another. The design and purpose, dusty as time. . . .

I recall with sadness the time when I moved with my two small children and their mother into a house at the south-western end of Western Native Township. A Sotho-speaking woman and her daughter watched us with silent suspicion. The family whose house we were occupying had been her friends for as long as she could remember. They had been forced to leave the house for a dwelling in an area that was later to become a part of Soweto.

'Look,' she said to a buxom woman leaning inquisitively over a fence, 'the Bushmen are already taking over our houses. We haven't even left and they are moving in over our heads.'

'I see them, they are just like vultures,' replied the buxom one. They conversed in Sesotho and did not seem to care whether or not we understood what they were saying. I resisted the urge to reply because I knew that she was wrong, and it hurt me to be called a Bushman. Instead I looked at them and smiled. They smiled back.

In the Cape Province which is heavily populated by coloureds, the Group Areas removals have been applied with merciless severity by the white government. Coloureds and Africans were driven off their lands and out of their homes in a grim display of power. Rich and fertile land was expropriated at low payouts to the coloureds and then resold to whites. Many property owners defied the orders to move but bulldozers broke their knees and their spirits. To defy bulldozers is to defy the god in whose name the machines speak and act. Roofs ripped apart while the occupants seek the respite of sleep from the harshness of the laws that govern their lives.

Ask any black person in any part of South Africa which of all the apartheid laws they detest most. First they will spit and then spit again; then they will tell you it is the dreaded Group Areas Act, cornerstone of apartheid — a law that has driven many to despair and even death. An Indian man in Sophiatown committed suicide when, after many court battles and a heavy drain on his finances, he was forced to leave his home in Tucker Street.

Thousands upon thousands of families have been uprooted from areas where their families have lived and died for many generations. There is no escape from the insatiable monster called the Group Areas Act.

It was therefore natural for that African woman to say: 'Look, the Bushmen are already taking over our houses.' It hurt, but I smiled.

Coloured people had said worse things about the whites. In Cape Town, they had actually attacked several government officials who ventured though the streets of their ill-fated District Six, which also waited in Group Areas death row, counting the days to its execution. And in Pretoria — the heart of Afrikanerdom and the place of execution — a simple and deeply religious Indian standowner, the now dead Nana Sita, was repeatedly jailed for refusing to move from his home of many generations. Sita, an indomitable believer in passive resistance, had been a close friend of Mahatma Gandhi during his years in the Transvaal. His refusal to obey unjust and ungodly laws was rooted in the teachings of Gandhi, and his determination to fight the government inspired and encouraged thousands of others. Sita's life ended a few hours after his release from prison during the late sixties. Few men in this world continue to live beyond their graves; Nana Sita was one of them. He had transformed despair into hope; fear into understanding; cowardice into courage.

Western Native Township was beyond Sophiatown and separated from it by a long, straight tarred road, tramlines, iron railings and several rows of pine trees. The railings stretched around the township with its matchbox shaped houses. There were two large gates, manned by several municipal police guards called blackjacks on account of their black uniforms. Many of these blackjacks assumed — and were later given — South African Government Police status. They became symbols of the white man's power and lived up to the reputation that the official constabulary had made for itself in the country. Western Native was built in 1919 or thereabouts as a transit camp for black migrants who came to Johannesburg to work in the municipal sewerage disposal department. The township ended up as the home of more than twenty thousand Africans who occupied the two thousand odd two-room brick houses, which had small yards with outside taps and toilets. But for a few strategically situated streets, the roads were untarred and remained in that condition long after the African people had been evicted and coloureds put into their houses.

And so, with Potgieter's words drumming in my ears, I ran to the home of my youngest and favourite uncle. 'Uncle Goon,' I said breathlessly, 'the Boers are going to demolish our houses tomorrow. I overheard the Dutchman Potgieter telling Abram of the shop.'

'So what, Donny. They have been breaking down the houses of thousands of families. What makes ours so special?' His words were cold and uncaring, but he was correct; demolitions were nothing new. The bulldozers had become a common sight and had moved against the Maimanes, Theunissens and Rathebes higher up in our buzzing street. I remember how the rich and respected Job Rathebe stood in bitter, angry silence while his luxurious house was torn apart. The attractive redbrick dwelling, where we had watched home movies and made eyes at the radiant and educated Rathebe sisters, tumbled with a roaring crash. Old man Rathebe removed his spectacles and dried his eyes.

Many such tears have flowed under the bridge of human tolerance since those painful years, and what my uncle so poignantly stated in his half-drunk stupor was true — other people's homes had also been destroyed.

True, only his words had been cold and uncaring. . . .

But Job Rathebe was a fighter, although in later years he was co-opted into the system of Bantu Councils. He was also director of a burial society and an insurance company, and owned several cars at the time. Before the bulldozers broke down his beautiful house, he put up a fight against the government in the Supreme Court, where he refused to be rushed out without being served with a notice to vacate his house, and demanded to be given a choice of houses at Diepkloof and Meadowlands. At a later hearing he submitted that the notice to vacate that he finally received was improper. His claim was upheld but that was by no means the end of the story. For who had ever heard of a 'kaffir' beating the white *baas* at his own game? Several appeals by the State were dismissed but the Boers had the last laugh. Job Rathebe died in 1983 in Soweto, alongside so many others who had refused to leave Sophiatown where, as African property-owners, they were among the elite of their day, envied and respected while others were despised and denigrated.

Two sides of the coin; this was Sophiatown. . . .

My uncle Goon shook his head several times and laughed: 'Donny, do those bloody houses really mean so much to you? I mean the best years of your life were spent in orphanages and at Catholic schools; why should it bother you so much?' He spoke softly, like someone who did not want to see his friend hurt. But I persisted: 'Let's go and tell Papa; pull out your car and let's drive to the old man. I'm sure that *he* would understand.' My uncle crept out from under the car he was fixing and wiped his forehead with the back of his greasy hand. He stared for a long time into my face and shook his head again. 'Go and get the keys,' he ordered.

We rode slowly through the embattled and besieged streets of Sophiatown, down the teeming Main Road, past the Newlands police station and into Albertsville. My grandpa, who rented a big house the state had bought from its coloured owner, was twiddling his thumbs and chewing on an unlit cigar. His favourite rocking chair was subdued and badly tattered. Whenever some fly ventured to sit on his lap, the old man instinctively grabbed his swat and, as usual, was off the mark. It was difficult to see his eyes because his broad-brimmed straw hat was pulled almost down to the bridge of his nose; no wonder he always missed the flies.

'Papa,' I said shakily, creating a brief moment of truce between him and the flies. 'Papa, the Dutch people are going to break down our houses tomorrow. Must we come to fetch you?' My voice had an anxious plea in it but he did not reply. When my uncle explained to him that newspaper reporters would be present to witness the demolition, the old man removed his moist cigar stub from his mouth and spat near the chair. It was deep-throated and final. The once proud owner of two large, comfortable houses and a massive yard, reduced to a mere tenant paying rent to the same state which would be destroying his homes.

Another throat-clearing act alerted me of impending vitriol: 'You *fok* off, me no come; why musta come? You thinka me want to see dat rubbish; no, me not come!' His booming voice fell into a sudden feeble croak: 'No Tatson you Papa no come.'

There was pain in his voice. Familiar like that which jabbed inside of me. I felt overwhelming pity for him as well as for myself. He drew the hat deeper over his face and sank into the chair humming his favourite Italian song, 'Tarantella'. He wasn't with us. We had shattered his peace and he was out searching for it. Then I pleaded with my uncle to take me to town; the newspapers would be interested in the story. Our houses, like our family, had a unique history which South Africa had to know. In the city, we discussed the issue with an African freelance reporter, Billy Leshabane who promised to write a piece. A few days after the demolition of our houses two Johannesburg daily newspapers carried stories about 'the houses with a difference'. But they didn't record the incident as I had witnessed it; they were not there at the time. . . .

On a Thursday in July 1962, a bleak sun rolled over my township shack and poured its liquid rays through the many tiny holes in the ceilingless roof. The African occupants, my predecessors, had maliciously ripped out the ceiling and destroyed the garden: no *Boesmans* were going to enjoy the fruits of their black labour. The rot of divide-and-rule had already set in. No Bushmen, when only a few days before, we had met and talked and laughed in the streets; 'their' children, 'our' children sharing the same hardships under separation and racial prejudice. 'Theirs' and 'ours'! God, what had happened to those bonds — those consanguine palpitations inside our breastbones?

The sunlight grew stronger and I tried to hold it as a gift for the unborn child — to be named Snowy after the snowfall that year — in my woman's womb.

It was an unusually bright day and the heat of the sun belied the fact that it was winter. My uncle Goon, whose face was covered in grease, called to his twelve-year-old son Raymond to hand him a set of spanners. My uncle reeked of liquor. 'So you want us to go and watch, eh?'

I nodded. We always conversed in broken Afrikaans; everybody in our family spoke Afrikaans. It was only with the old man that we communicated in a sort of English. Sometimes my father and his brothers addressed the old man in his own language, especially when we had Italian visitors. The Boers called our brand of Afrikaans *kombuistaal* (kitchen language). It was spoken by domestic workers and to the Boers it was a denigration and bastardisation of Afrikaans. This *taal* gave direct birth to the township patois called *tsotsi taal*, the colloquial lingo of the thugs and won't-work layabouts who preyed first on the whites, and later attacked and robbed their own people.

The bulldozing had not begun. All the familiar bearings were still there; the apple, fig and plum trees waited bare and sullen. Our huge grapevine, with its gnarled and calloused arms, stood like a freak, rejected and barren.

But when the leaves were green and moist, and the vines full and heavy with black grapes, how happy was my grandpa then; singing and laughing like the Neapolitan lad in the vineyards of southern Italy. He had a huge wooden vat smeared on the outside with tar which he filled with grapes. He ordered us to wash our feet and crush the fruit for a small payment. It was interesting to be a part of the wine-making, through the fermenting period and the using of cotton bags in place of the traditional wine-press, right up to the final bottling.

When the leaves were green and moist, how sweet were the grapes of our contentment in the place we called home.

The wood and coal shed, once the home of dozens of pigeons, had already been partly damaged by the manual demolition squad whose heavy mallets had caused several bruises and scars on the walls. Its huge wooden doors had been removed by human scavengers or the state storeman. For either party, the doors would fetch a tidy price. Our two houses were also doorless and the heavy window-frames had been removed. Children and grown-ups used to scavenge like vultures over the corpses of demolished houses for valuables. Doors, ceilings, iron gates, awnings and window-frames brought in good prices for the unemployed people. Many people also cleaned and sold bricks to construction firms with or without the consent of the government authorities. Hawkers and hardware stores did a roaring trade from the destruction.

There's a saying in Afrikaans which goes: *Een man se dood is 'n ander man se stukkie brood* which means that one man will gain from another's misfortune. I was among a group of young scavengers. We used to move from one executed house to another, street by street, to rip up the wooden flooring in our hunt for hidden treasure, especially those legendary tins of old gold coins said to have been left behind by some ancient black miser.

Sometimes the finds would be gruesome and shocking: the skeleton of an unwanted child, the remains of a murdered person, the animal skins and bones of a witchdoctor. Money carried no omen even if it was found in the palm of a skeleton. The houses were destroyed and then ransacked by the victims themselves. This was the unnatural order of things beyond the control of the African people. Or so it seemed at the time. So had it been with the homes of others and so would it be with ours. Sadness and bad luck, say the African elders, walk in queues. What they actually mean is that they come in turns.

The old well, in its early pre-War days, had given the family its much needed water supply when other families had to buy water from the municipal authorities in the adjoining Western Native Township. Now it was filled with stones and debris. It had also been the storage place for our watermelons and was the spot where, as a six-year-old, I had watched my uncle Giovanni collapse and die of a heart-attack. He had gasped for air and with his hands around his throat, 'call ma,' he whispered in Afrikaans, 'call ma. . . .' Then his body jerked violently up and down. Up and then down for the last time. It was the first time I had watched a member of my family die. Many more were to follow. I lifted his head onto my lap and stroked it gently.

Death was to become a frequent visitor to our family. The well had indeed bitter and sweet memories for me. The two big kennels that had housed our dogs Bruno and Rover were broken up and the planks neatly piled for some family's firewood needs. And as we moved around the spacious yard, my uncle, his wife and their son appeared unmoved by my honing. A mischievous wind swirled in a circle and took with it many dry leaves which swayed like bronze ballerinas in the golden July sunlight. The leaves danced to their own music and soared higher and higher into the air and over the jagged bottle-topped walls to vanish from sight. Voices and sounds I knew from my childhood and feared in my youth, echoed from the swirling dust. Familiar voices that spoke of those days and nights I had spent in my grandfather's house and in his warm bed. No thought ever that he was an immigrant with an upbringing and history so strong, it was always reflected in his character and actions. And he never rejected or demeaned his coloured family.

The voices and sounds that had echoed in the streets of Sophiatown before the apartheid warlords came with their death machines and ordered us out of our homes, rang in my ears and in an onslaught of nostalgia and longing. But the heavy growling noise of two approaching bulldozers stirred my daydreaming.

The time of execution had come for our homes like it had for so many thousands before ours. Throughout the country, cosmopolitan townships — the antithesis of separation and racial prejudice — were being wounded and felled by the crushing blows of the white man's laws. So it was then, so it is now.

The vehicles were driven by two Boers who each had an African attendant sitting behind them as if they were apprentice bulldozers. Job reservation was not whittling away, this was just Verwoerd's policy of letting the African do his dirty work. The machines began their destruction. My eyes were fixed on my grandparents' house. One of the killers attacked the kitchen, leaving a gaping wound in its side. Beaten and battered, the kitchen collapsed and died. One machine stopped; it appeared to be bracing itself for another onslaught. It revved incessantly, its teeth and jaws locked. Then, in one mad rush, it rammed viciously into the old folks' bedroom, so that the walls collapsed and raised a blinding cloud of dust. The room was flattened.

I saw particles of blood and bone that were not visible to the naked eye; not, anyway, to the dust-filled eyes of my relatives. A strange indescribable sadness came over me, like the sensation that comes to the skin when an insect crawls over it; or the sudden shudder at the sight of a decaying corpse.

For the African people the bedrooms of their parents inspire a certain reverence. One never just sat on their beds without permission. It was one of many customs and unwritten codes of conduct that found and manifested themselves in our coloured family.

The assault continued. Blow after blow. The house began to crumble and the roof sagged to one side. My half-drunk uncle shouted something to the driver about the stuffed springbok head above the front door that we had apparently forgotten to remove. But no sooner had he spoken than the horns were crushed beneath the machine. My uncle swore and cursed at the man, who switched off the bulldozer and angrily told us he had no time to be on the lookout for springbok heads. How the man had heard the cursing was beyond me, but he responded: 'Listen *boetie*, I'm only doing my job.'

Just a job; just hired killers, nothing more.

The bulldozing continued. The two pillars I had often climbed to reach the roof fell towards us and cracked into several pieces, like bones breaking. I looked beyond the pillars and the dust; they symbolised the falling apart and subjugation of our family, of our township and its people. When the roof eventually collapsed, I realised that bulldozers could take apart in a few minutes all that had been built up over the years; over generations and generations of children.

The power to destroy and the pain of being destroyed. . . . Dust. I looked again and I was a child once more, pushing an old bicycle wheel around our houses, under the plum- and fig-trees, beneath the strong grapevine — a child listening to familiar sounds: rich Neapolitan songs, fragments of our Italian heritage, coming from the piano-accordions of my two uncles. And my folks were with me amid the noise and dust of the bulldozers.

Flashes of that cruel day when the first removals started in Sophiatown crossed my mind. Sophiatown, the trouble-spot and 'nest of communist agitators', where the oppressed people didn't take things lying down and where cheeky 'kaffirs', '*Boesmans*' and 'coolies' retaliated against police brutality and aggression. It was one township that had offered resistance to the apartheid system and the lie that, as a *herrenvolk*, the Boers had been anointed to lead the darker, and therefore lesser, creatures of God to salvation and civilisation. It was the legacy of their forefathers — won with the blood of sacrifice and endurance, their Christian calling — to lead the tribes out of the bondage and sin of a new Sodom and Gomorrah called Sophiatown. Go it had to, even at the cost of human lives. For that was what the *volk* wanted, and Verwoerd was a servant of the *volk*, nothing more. . . .

The new place that would rise out of her ashes would be called 'the place of triumph'— Triomf — which embodied all that the Boers stood for and would ostensibly gain when the last black person was removed from Sophiatown. The triumph was etched on the weapons of those who represented and defended the regime. The triumph was manifested in the division the white government and its allies had sown among the inhabitants of Sophiatown, so that many Africans lost confidence in their Indian and coloured counterparts who were to be left behind, however temporarily. The triumph also echoed from Verwoerd's vow that he would destroy Sophiatown and erase it from the memory of its people. And he was a servant of the *volk* nothing more.

Government-supporting stooges and propagandists spoke of the promise of good things in Meadowlands. There would be many new schools and recreation centres for the children; halls where the inhabitants could meet and discuss their problems with the white rulers. There would be better security and the safety of the law-abiding would be ensured. The vicious threats of tsotsism and gangsterism would be eliminated and above all, the African people would no longer suffer at the hands of the shrewd Jew and the leeching Indian. The coloureds would be sent to their own areas, for that was what they had always wanted. It was also the law.

The law of divide and rule. Old as time itself.

I may have been too young to comprehend the power of those forces that were driving wedges between the oppressed people at the time, but I saw and felt their effects on the people of Sophiatown. Africans, Indians and coloured people who for many, many years had lived together harmoniously alongside Chinese and a sprinkling of white immigrant families, were being wilfully driven apart. The weak fell prey to propaganda, and racial hostility won the day.

Separation was to become a way of life. As the Boer churches preached heavily against miscegenation, warning that the offspring of such illicit love-making adventures would be moronic and a curse to mankind. Genetics proved this, they claimed, and above all, God would not lie.

He was on the side of truth and what they said was true.

Hitler had also believed this. . . .

The people moved and took with them all their broken dreams; all their high expectations and hopes and the fragments of things dear and prized. I looked on helplessly as many of my best friends, and my enemies too, boarded the army trucks with their families. They waved and laughed mechanically — many were not aware of the full political implications of their exodus. Those who were cried uncontrollably as we kissed and hugged.

The prospect of a new home and a private lavatory, even if it was built outside in the yard, was more than a man could ask for, so the people were told. There would be privacy — something countless mothers and fathers had always prayed for in the ghettos. Middle-class Africans would be able to buy land in Diepkloof and build their own homes. It would be a Houghton of the African areas with all the modern municipal services of any white suburb. Meadowlands would be a paradise of peace and song.

And the people longed for peace — any kind of peace, as long as they could escape the invasion of the Union Defence Force and the police, who had surrounded and raided their homes and arrested their loved ones. They were sickened by the constant bickering among the white parliamentarians for and against the government, on what was good for the African people. They were also disheartened by their own divided and disorganised political leaders who spoke about revolution and liberation but failed to deliver the goods; failed to answer violence with violence. What was there left for them but song, songs of sadness and joy sung as only the African people sing, from the deep sap of their beings.

The great removal was in the winter of 1955, and since then many people have told the story of Sophiatown. But there remains that unwritten manuscript; the untold story of a boy fighting in the streets, a boy who was once secure in his dreams before destruction came to his city, to his family and to himself.

This is my story. . . .

2. Bad News

*A*ccording to the racial statistics of South Africa, I am a second generation coloured: the fruit of miscegenation and an in-between existence; the appendage of black and white. There are approximately four million other people like me — twilight children who live in political, social and economic oblivion and who have been cut off from the mainstream of direct interaction with both black and white people. But many coloured people, especially adults, have looked to the whites for their survival and security. There has been a rapid move by the younger, more radical people towards political and social integration with blacks because of the success of the black consciousness movement in South Africa. After the removal of people from cosmopolitan areas such as Sophiatown, the Verwoerdian protagonists — political scientists and academics — obviously with the collaboration of many coloured quislings, have created a middle-class among the coloureds. And, employing the *swartgevaar* (black danger) slogan, they have drawn many twilight people closer to the white laager. Closer but not into it. Just close enough to serve as a buffer between white and black, and the latter are slowly beginning to doubt the bona fides of their lighter-skinned brothers and sisters.

It is only in this mad and frightened portion of the world, bedevilled as it is by race consciousness and pigmentocracy, that human beings are categorised and classified under the law into sub-tribal and sub-human units. Consider the coloureds. The Griquas are the so-called descendants of an aboriginal chief called Adam Kok whose land was first seized by the British colonialists and later the Boers following unsuccessful uprisings against both the occupying forces of his day. Adam Kok's territory inside the borders of South Africa is still known as Griqualand.

Then there are the Cape coloureds — the name denotes a direct genetic link with the so-called Bushmen and Hottentots — preferably known as the Khoisan. What the segregationists could not escape was that so many of these Bushman and Hottentot offspring had blue, grey or green eyes with straight blond hair. The other Cape 'mixture' is known as Cape Malay. Although a large section of this grouping has traces of Malayan blood, many thus classified are very light-skinned, with European features as well as Khoisan characteristics. The original Malay slaves were brought into South Africa by the Dutch East India Company settlers, the majority of whom did not bring women with them. The other lesser known coloured 'tribes' are the 'Maasbieker', the name being derived from the word Mozambique and meaning 'a type of Mozambique coloured'. There are the 'Basters' or Bastards — half-breeds, mainly found in South West Africa/Namibia and in parts of the Northern Cape Province. The Mauritian coloureds, most of them light-skinned and long-haired, are chiefly based in South Africa's Natal Province and choose English as their language, unlike their counterparts in the Transvaal and the Cape who mostly speak Afrikaans. Perhaps the most obnoxious and the most hated label is 'Other coloureds' — referring to 'mixtures' that possibly arose out of relationships outside the white group, such as the offspring of African and Chinese, African and Indian, and African and all the other aforementioned coloured varieties.

Where did it all begin for me?

We stood in a long queue inside a state-owned courtyard waiting our turns to be classified or reclassified either as 'pure' coloureds or as 'natives' — as Africans were officially dubbed in the forties and fifties. As a flower or tree would be classified into a certain species, so were the coloureds grouped and regrouped, until they stopped believing they were just humans. For it is in the nature of men to create pigeon-holes. When I left the classroom at the Vrededorp High School, in the company of several of my standard eight classmates one day in August 1955, it was by order of an Act of the white parliament which decreed that all 'coloureds' or even so-called coloureds were to report to specially set up reclassification courts to determine our 'race'.

William 'Lovely-boy' Bokera, a very yellow-skinned boy, who like me had an African mother and a coloured father, tugged nervously at my jacket sleeve. The sweat of the fear of the unknown glistened on his forehead like oil. 'Hey Don, are we going to tell the fokking Boere that our old ladies are darkies? I mean it's not their bloody business who our damned mothers are; I mean we didn't tell our *toe-jappes* (fathers) to grab darkie *ousies* (girls).' I didn't answer. There's no way I was going to reply; one never knew who else was in the yard, keenly watching and recording speeches and events.

'Hey, are you listening, bra? Are we going to tune them about our old ladies?'

'I don't know, Lovely-boy but it shouldn't really matter because as I understand it you are what your father is, and in our cases, both our fathers are half-white and they have not been classified native or African,' I said, trying to allay his fears.

'Never! In this country you are what they think you should be, what they want you to be, and all that through the stroke of a pen. Since this reclassification shit, everyone is changing his surname.'

I nodded. How widespread it was this conversion of surnames. Sonnyboy Letlapa (Stone in Tswana), who was a fair-skinned Morolong, changed his surname to Kleppers derived from the Afrikaans word *klippe* (stones). Direct adaptations were Maybee from Mabe; Radbee from Radebe; Cummings from Khumalo and McKwenna from Mokwena; the list is endless.

Some people actually adopted our surname. Once a policeman

called at our home to inform us that one of our relations — one B. Mattera — had been arrested for a pass offence. I hurried down thinking it was my father because his initials were B.G. I saw a man called Basil inside the prison courtyard. I enquired whether he had seen my father because our information was that a B. Mattera had been arrested. He smiled sheepishly, almost remorsefully, and said: 'I hope you don't mind Donny, but I gave them my name as Basil Mattera.' I shook my head. 'You do recall,' he added, 'that I used to work for your folks. Please tell that Boer over there I'm your uncle!' His voice fell to a pleading whisper.

'*Meneer,*' I said to the obese desk sergeant, 'that man over there is my uncle. He's a coloured; can you please release him?'

The policeman shook with derisive bursts of laughter. 'That kaffir your uncle? Don't tickle my arse. Since when do Hotnots slice open their ears? Just look at that blerry *houtkop* (wooden head); a real *fokken* Zulu with only painted wooden plugs missing in his ears. If he's your uncle, then I was the blerry midwife!' His laughter rang through my ears, into my stomach and fell deep into the soles of my feet.

Lovely-boy Bokera's father, who was also known as Bokeer, had won respect as an outstanding golfer and a man who had a way with women. His wife Nana was a simple, buxom Tswana who had not lost her rural traditional traits nor ever hid or was ashamed of her blackness. This, apparently, was the cause of Lovely-boy's uneasiness — that he might, like hundreds before him, be reclassified African. The queue was shortening; some men emerged in tears and others smiling. A tear and a smile; out of one 'race' and into another by the stroke of a pen and through the scrutinous eyes of Afrikaner officialdom. I shuddered at the thought of being made a 'native' overnight without having a say in the matter although, because of my close connection with my Tswana relatives, I felt no shame about being an African.

Suddenly a group of men in front of Lovely-boy and me moved out of the queue to speak to a man at the exit point of the reclassification office. Amid quiet whispers and the shaking of heads, I detected concern on their faces. One by one they moved towards the huge gates, all of them touching their hair.

I approached one of them. 'Excuse me big man, what's happening? Why are you guys all pulling your hair like that and where are you going?'

'To the barber-shop, boy; we're all dashing out for a haircut!'

'Why?'

Pointing over his shoulder with his thumb, he said: 'Those bastards in there, those dogs are using matchsticks and pens to classify us!'

'Matchsticks? Pens?'

'Yes,' came the quick response. 'Matchsticks and *fokken* pens, which they run through our hair! And when the pen or matchstick gets stuck, the Boers shout: "Go to Room 47 and get a pass!" Like we were *fokken* natives. What the hell do they take us for?'

His words stung everyone into silence. People began looking at each other's heads. Those with soft, straight hair smiled confidently and one or two actually combed their heavily-greased hair to the open envy of some of the more curly-haired, who were now vanishing from the queue. A very dark-skinned man smiled quietly. He had shaved off all his hair: matchsticks and pens cannot get stuck on a bald head. A tear or a smile on the way to pain and humiliation or to the joy and satisfaction of being a 'real' coloured.

Lovely-boy emerged a 'pure' coloured. He had passed all the tests without a single hitch: he could recite both the Lord's Prayer and Psalm 23 in Afrikaans; exclaimed *'eina!'* (ouch) and not 'aychoo' as a 'native' would when inflicted with sudden pain. Lovely-boy was a few inches taller as he walked through the heavy gates. My turn came.

'And what do you want to be, *boetie?*' said *meneer* Lotter, my classifier. 'A Hotnot or an Italian? I see your whole family has already been issued with identity numbers; yours must be in the batch.' There had been no matchsticks or pens; no blood tests, no scrutiny. I was the Italian's son, and the last-born of the family. If the Boers believed I was my grandpa's son, I was not going to be the one to shatter that belief. My number was 331-591697C; the 'C' stood for coloured but the birth certificate read 'mixed' in the column denoting race. It was the first I knew of a race called mixed. Mixed, though, was far far better than native, and being called kaffir, as many reclassified coloureds were to discover. Heart-rending stories, filled with biting humiliation and anguish, daily made newspaper headlines in the late fifties. Some victims of the reclassification trauma chose suicide to bail them out of their absurd misery. Whole and stable families were shattered overnight as brothers, sisters, sons and daughters were ripped apart by the cruel laws of race separation. Relentless pass raids netted in hundreds of 'borderline' cases; those bordering between African and coloured, not between white and coloured. The latter species would be dealt with only later as the 'other coloured' grouping.

In one sordid instance of reclassification insanity in 1955 Thomas Wentzel an elderly man in Noordgesig, Johannesburg, was also reclassified native when he approached the authorities to ask why his son William had been reclassified. Old man Wentzel had fought against the Germans in two wars, a coloured soldier in the Cape Coloured Corps.

The dark- and fair-skinned Gabriel brothers were split; one to 'pure' and the other to 'native' pigeon-holes and never the twain to meet in the same township or the same house. This was the Law.

A comb once stuck in the hair of a man called Maynard in a reclassification office in 1955, and presto, a 'native' was born. His cranium, the shape of his nose and lips and forehead, were minutely scrutinised and compared against the government-approved human charts and genetic diagrams; their authenticity, power and finality were indisputable.

And where there is power there is corruption. The two are inseparable, like twins joined in the womb. There was no price too high nor gift too expensive to bend and twist laws that forced people to live lies and demean themselves in the land of their fathers. Men and women hid in fear of pass arrests, tasting for once a small measure of the anguish and the shame that were part of the lives of the millions of Africans throughout the country.

And, as the law of the white man would have it, many of these unfortunate creations of God — in a way creations of the god apartheid — have accepted the categorisations without any real protest. Into this group called coloured, this cultureless genetic enigma, was I classified 'for the purposes of the South African Population Register'. But in their heart of hearts the Boers know this is only one of the many offerings they make at the altar of their god.

With the stroke of a pen, my Africanness and the acquired Italian tradition of my paternal grandfather were obliterated. Apartheid decided my race and my destiny on that dusty August day of 1955 in a government courtyard, where men stood in long queues to be branded and pedigreed with the hot iron of humiliation and scorn. Second-class citizens with a second-class future and destiny; South Africa's dirt-heap race; or so the people were made to see themselves.

My mother, Dinki Agnes Lebakeng, was born of simple and strongly traditional Barolong (a Tswana tribe) parents, whose own parents came from a place near Bechuanaland called Rama Habama, and had trekked down through Mafikeng to the sprawling frontier of the Golden City — which had attracted people of many shades and ethnic affiliations with the promise and hope of jobs and homes.

My maternal grandparents lived in the old sparsely populated Johannesburg area of Troyeville where my mother's elder sisters and brother were born. With the establishment of the Village Main gold mine, the Lebakeng family moved to the now dead Prospect Township on the outskirts of the city. Three other Lebakeng children were born there amid the squalor and poverty peculiar to transit camps and labour dormitories where work-seeking migrants pitched tents and makeshift structures. It was in late December of 1920 — and fifteen years before my own birth — that my mother opened her eyes in a house of dire poverty and suffering in Troye Street. Two years before she was born, one of her mother's male relatives had been severely beaten up for performing scab labour as a remover of buckets of human waste during a strike in Johannesburg by African municipal workers over a demand for higher pay.

My African family then moved to Western Native Township where I was born on December 29, 1935. After a few years they moved to Sophiatown. I was named Monnapula — Tswana for 'the-man-who-came-with-the-rain'. According to the folklore of the African people, my birth had been a good omen because it came after a long and damaging drought and hunger which had gripped the land.

I was parted from my mother. She was forced to return to what is known among black people as 'the kitchens'. She worked for some white family in one of the affluent areas of Johannesburg. My father's people all loved her. She was beautiful, with lovely sleek legs and a body to match. Snookie, a man I knew well, used to call her 'English Lady'. I cannot recall whether she and my father had ever lived together or even strolled hand-in-hand in the moonlight. My father was a handsome womaniser who had many African women as lovers and common-law wives. He had good taste: they were beautiful. Yet with all their apartness I still loved both my parents I guess.

I also loved all my grandparents. To me, having a European grandpa was no different from having a Tswana one. I mean, which child then would have noticed what most children — especially the white ones — are alert to now? There were real differences of course. One household had more food than the other and it must have been natural for me to favour the house where food was abundant. Game, fruit, salads and delicious Italian dishes smiled appetisingly from my grandparents' dinner table. There was enough wood and coal. And there was money.

My grandfather, Francesco Paulo Mattera, came to South Africa from Naples, Italy, in 1904. He was twenty-six and a sailor in the merchant navy. His parents were farmers and his taste for adventure, which began with street singing, led him to the shores of Cape Town. He jumped ship, and after roaming friendless through the city, met my grandmother, Minnie Rawana, a narrow-eyed beauty of Xhosa-Dutch and Griqua extraction with a copper-coloured skin. They married at a Dutch mission at Graaff-Reinet, the birthplace of my grandmother.

There was no law against marriage between black and white in South Africa then. They loved each other and that was all that mattered. My grandfather often told us, 'Dat time, no beeznees lika now. You marreed who you marreed. Nobaady he say who dis man or dat womman. No law to breakka a man an his womman. . . .'

He often spoke about how the colour bar was becoming a law unto itself and how it would someday even prevent people from living together because of racial preservation. 'Me, I marreed your mudda becozza I luva her, not becozza me white man and she a black womman. Dutch man (the Boers) he not ta white.' His words never really struck home, not until I was infatuated with what I thought was love for a girl called Poppy, who lived with her coloured mother and white father in the township of Westdene, where many poor whites lived. Westdene was separated from the bustling Sophiatown by Toby Street where, as young children, we fought and played with the Boer children. The 'nonnas', as the white girls were called by their servants, were our favourite targets, which always displeased their brothers and sparked fights. It was good fun at the time, but in later years I came to realise and experience the near-fatal danger of making eyes at white girls. They were holy ground, the strength and pride of the white nation. It did not matter at the time whether the white girl loved you or not.

My grandparents travelled from Cape Town to Kimberley where they found a few small diamonds, and finally settled in the Transvaal, in the heart of the booming Golden City. Together they started a small business, selling in typical Italian fashion hot dogs, hamburgers, popcorn, peanuts and balloons. Then my grandpa took a job on the mines. Many Africans became his friends, but they knew their place, he would tell us. 'In my contree eez no white, eez no black — only rich and poor.' He said they would not believe his wife was black. The only African miner who did was Jim. He and my grandpa became inseparable. Jim had been attracted to the old man's barrel-organ and clever chimpanzee, which thrilled the simple-minded white and African miners. Jim also loved my two aunts and my father. When Jim left the mine to work for my grandparents he was given a good pair of second-hand mine boots as a reward for his loyalty. My grandpa told me that the barefooted Jim nearly died of delight.

'Jim, he no wear da boots. He clean wid polish to shine like da sun. He tied around neck and walk wid barefeet. Stones break da toes but Jim no wear. "Why you no wear, Jim?" I say. "New meat can grow for da feet, but not new leadda for da boots," Jim say. . . .'

My 'Papa', as I called my grandpa, built two large cottages in Gerty Street. Transport was a problem in early Johannesburg and in those days anyone could own or start a bus company. Ours was called Morosina, after my grandpa's mother. Money flowed in and difficulties arose among my uncles and aunts. The old man left the mines after nineteen years because of partial blindness and sickness — and retired into business.

Sometimes he reminisced about his country and his people, and their history of war and peace. But so thick, like a swelling river, flowed the music of his land in his veins, that when he sang a lump instantly came to his throat. The choking was gentle. I traced tears of longing and nostalgia in his half-blind eyes. Through them I virtually lived in the farm cottage in his native Italy, and walked among the olive trees eating as I sang. It was my feet that crushed the grapes to make wine, my hands that ground the wheat and harvested potatoes. Even my blood was shed in the long vendettas. I became one with them who I had never seen or touched or spoken to.

For many months after my grandmother's funeral, and later when I returned to Johannesburg from the Durban Catholic convent school, my grandpa talked about my grandma, about the way they had lived, her cooking, the way she walked and spoke. Most of all it was her narrow eyes that smiled when they had to cry, he said. He told us of his deep love for her. There had been many, many women, beautiful white women, but he had chosen her. It was a pity, he said, that his parents in Italy had not lived to see her.

I spent my childhood in poverty among my African relatives. Apparently my paternal coloured granny was informed of my plight and came to fetch me. My mother was home at the time and I recall how my African cousins, Dutch and Panini, cried as they helped pack my bags. I was leaving them for greener and richer pastures; for a house of plenty. My invalid Kuku, as I called my Tswana grandmother, gripped me tightly after I had kissed and said goodbye. She refused to let go and shouted my African name: 'Monnapula, Monnapula.' It was a parting that I will remember as long as I live. But I often returned to see her and brought money and food from my new, affluent home, where I learned new ways and spoke better Afrikaans and a bit of English. I had become a coloured — something I was truly unconscious of until the removals of Sophiatown. My Kuku always laughed when I told her about my new environment. On the one day I didn't visit her, I was told that she had died. Lightning had struck the old pine tree in front of her yard and it had rained heavily that night. Her last words had been for me.

My mother visited me on certain Thursdays when, like many other domestic workers she was allowed a day off. I have pleasant memories of those visits. She would bring me new clothes and toys and sweets. And always, when it came to parting, tears failed to soothe the deep longing and love I had for her. Sometimes I felt deserted and rejected although my paternal granny tried to fill the vacuum with kind deeds. She taught me to be strong, and I grew to love her profoundly. I called her Ma-Minnie.

The Mattera family were as cosmopolitan as Sophiatown itself, and the sons of wealthy Italian immigrant families used to call on my father's two elder sisters, Rosina and Helena, with a view to marriage. Rosina who was called Rosie, married Francisco Perreira, a very light-skinned coloured of Portuguese extraction. Their only son Frank who was nicknamed Koukie had dark, Indian features but strongly resembled his father. But father and son were to each other as fire is to water — always arguing, always clashing over religion or money which the father loved and worshipped. Koukie was literally and figuratively the black sheep of his family and lived up to it through the bottle, through women and through gambling. He worked as a bookkeeper but was arrested after he had defrauded the company of thousands of pounds. He was acquitted on a technicality.

Koukie had nothing to show for his life and drank liquor as if it came from a tap in his backyard. Women could not live with him because of his violent temper. Two suicide attempts were thwarted by his paternal first cousin Norah whom he married against his father's protestations based on biblical authority. He and I were very close — we shared secrets, money, food and books — but not close enough I guess. I found him hanging behind his bedroom door, his tongue protruding over his lips and his eyes wide as two full moons. The house was in total darkness at the time and the match I had lighted and held in cold astonishment burned my fingers. I ran outside in sheer disbelief but returned to embrace him as he swung from the leather belt he had tied around the coat-hook on the door. He felt a bit warm, alive. There was no suicide note, only a book at his feet with a marker. When I finally opened the book I found several sentences that told of sorrow and fear ringed in red ink: that sorrow was better than fear; that sorrow at least was an arriving whereas fear was a journey — a terrible journey.

But the fear and sorrow that Alan Paton wrote about in his classic *Cry the Beloved Country* was different from that which cousin Koukie had experienced in his lonely and terribly mixed up life. For whatever sorrow my cousin may have felt, he never showed or spoke about it to anyone in the family. He always warned me not to trust people, especially women — his mother included. His parents had moved from Sophiatown to the elite coloured township of Albertsville which lay in a valley surrounded to the north and west by the white areas of Northcliff and Newlands. Albertsville's close proximity to whites gave a false respectability to its residents, who consequently looked down on shack dwellers. Cousin Koukie's parents became snobs — something he hated vehemently because of his intimate relationships with Africans at all levels. Most of his girlfriends were African and he openly dissociated himself from people showing any pro-coloured or pro-white tendencies.

Koukie was addicted to reading and possessed a powerful English and Afrikaans vocabulary, which enabled him to enter several crossword puzzle competitions with great success. Our wealthy grandpa also gave him a weekly cash allowance that he spent on horse-racing. His mother, a real smart dresser with a touch of class, would sometimes give him money on the sly because his father was a hard, born-again Christian who, unlike his master Jesus Christ, had no time for beggars. And as far as Mr Perreira was concerned, his son was a beggar — an unrepentant prodigal who refused to say: 'Father I have sinned. . . .'

Aunt Helena my father's second sister, was known as Baby. She was named after one of my grandfather's sisters in Italy and had married a white motor mechanic and former racing driver, a Scotsman called Albert Fernhold. Their only son, also Albert, had such 'white' features — blue-green eyes and blond hair — that most African and coloured kids called him 'Laanie' — a colloquial term meaning both European and wealthy. We called him Chossie. He was terribly spoilt, and was allowed to drive cars and ride motorcycles at an early age, and had a mechanical mind like his father. Chossie, like Koukie, moved to Western Native Township after our families were ordered to leave Sophiatown. He died in a mental institution.

We learned later that his eyes, heart and kidneys had been used for transplants. His was one funeral service in our family that I could not attend because permission to do so was refused as I was, in the government's parlance, a restricted person — banned from attending all public gatherings under the dreaded Prohibition of Communism Act of 1950. But that is another story. . . .

My uncle Willie, fourth of my grandparents' children, lived with an exquisitely beautiful white woman called Tilly who had sleek long hair that fell over her left eye like the famous actress Veronica Lake. She was always elegantly dressed. Tilly and my grandma got on quite well. When uncle Willie joined the South African army to fight against the Germans, it was the last we saw of our lovely Tilly.

My other three uncles, Danny, Frankie and Goon lived with many African, coloured and Indian women whom I had to address as

Aunt. I understood. My father too brought many different women to his room. There was the African nurse, whom I liked best. She was beautiful and kind, giving me the best things and always standing up for me whenever I had done something wrong. In a sense my coloured family was symbolic of the cosmopolitan complexion of Sophiatown. Other families also had white fathers and African or coloured mothers. There were the Bairds, Rosenbergs, Rutherfords, Theunissens, Janowskis, Jansens, Haupts, the Ryans, the Fitzgeralds and a host of others who shared the teeming, vibrant township alongside thousands of racially mixed inhabitants — many of whom were helped to birth through my grandma's skills as a midwife. Ordinary people, living together, dying together.

My granny became a household name. I often accompanied her on her midwifery rounds and carried the little black bag that always contained some liquor, which she called medicine. Sometimes, when she had had too much of the medicine, she would walk very unsteadily. On such nights, many a mother underwent double pain. My granny usually walked very briskly. Her eyes were bright and when she laughed — as she so often did — a dimple cuddled neatly in the side of her face. She couldn't speak English well; she and my grandpa communicated partly in Italian and partly in broken English. She was an expert cook and mastered every dish my grandpa taught her, as well as the art of wine making. My granny demanded complete respect from her children for herself and her husband. She never hesitated to fling a plate, a knife or a heavy iron at any sign of disobedience. My father's loyalty to his parents was unquestionable.

I would like to think that the Mattera clan was indeed a real and living part of Sophiatown; for if there was death in some poor family, Go to Mattera — or Matticks, as the African people called my grandpa. If someone needed bail money, Go to Mattera — the people with the buses and the cars — they always give. There was food aplenty. Cripples and beggars, some in tattered disguise, came for their weekly rations. The not-so-rich white people; government officials and high-ranking policemen, never left empty-handed and always tried their best to return the favours. This was the generous nature of my family — and it was Sophiatown's way of life. This was the family that took me from my poor, struggling Tswana kith and kin and helped to form part of my childhood dreams.

3. To Become a Man

*J*anuary 1943. I stood in front of my paternal granny's dressing-table, almost transfixed. The multi-coloured cap on my head was perched very quaintly to one side. The grey suit was tightly buttoned. I had just turned seven and I was going to a Roman Catholic convent school — Saint Theresa's — in Mayville, Durban in Natal. The old woman had busied herself packing my clothes and lunch-basket. She would pinch me softly now and then and I could feel the love with which she touched me. When I was disobedient, the pinching was violent. This time her soft hands rubbed my cheeks and her snuff-smelling mouth kissed the tears of parting from my eyes.

'Don't cry, my baby,' she said in Afrikaans. 'You are going to become a man. Indication is the only gift I can give you.' Indication was the word she used for education.

'You take a good watch, Tatson,' urged my grandpa, calling me by a nickname that actually meant 'Tarzan' because of my ability to climb trees and rooftops. I held firmly to both of them and cried.

'Don't cry. Don't worry,' she coaxed. 'Ma will be waiting for her little man when he comes back from school.'

But this was not to be. The kissing and the holding and the coaxing would be the last for me. She died while I was at school.

My mother accompanied me to Johannesburg station and I held on to her as if it would also be the last time she and I would be together. My mother was radiant and beautifully dressed, and as I sat in my compartment I heard my father hum his favourite tune — the wartime Vera Lynn song 'You'll Never Know'. It was a song I loved because it always reminded me of my uncle Willie who had enlisted to fight the Germans.

My mother and father saw me off at the station. For once they were together, holding hands and laughing. This was a new experience, one that I had always longed for. I wished they would stay happily together forever. My mother stuffed three pounds into my pocket, kissed me several times and told me to take care.

'Men don't kiss,' my father said, and so we shook hands. I too was going to be a man. Everybody was so sure that I was going to be a man. In those days we believed our parents unquestioningly. When they said you were going to be a man you accepted it. Perhaps it was sheer dreaming, the kind that sustains against futility and despair, when a parent hopes to God that his son will become a man, with the dignity the word implies.

I truly loved my parents although much of my life was spent away from them. As people thronged around the coach I saw, for the first time in my life, my father and mother hold hands and suddenly kiss in full view of the public. The whistle sounded and people eager to leave the coach hustled and pushed nervously. My mother squeezed another three pounds into my hand and kissed me on the mouth. My father, born a few blocks away from this very railway station, a six footer with curly brown hair and grey eyes who commanded much respect in Sophiatown, told me again that men never kissed. He just shook my hand. He had once been a member of the underworld, jailed and assaulted on many occasions.

There was something about him that I feared: he knew all there was to know. He had seen and felt everything about life, people said he was a law unto himself. A man who had abandoned my mother when she was carrying me, and had brought women to our house. This man whom I loved so deeply but had never had the courage to tell, gripped my hand firmly.

'Remember, Zinga,' he said, calling me by his own nickname. 'Remember you are going to school to become a man.'

It was final.

I told myself I wouldn't disappoint him or my granny. A man I was surely going to become. My mother nodded and smiled. The world was a great place and I felt important as my father kissed her again. The nurse and his other women hardly crossed my mind. Then, amid the last goodbyes, the see-you-agains and God-bless-yous; amid the tears and hugs and the hot kisses, the train jerked violently and moved away. My parents were still holding hands as if to reassure me of their love. Then they became specks along with the other people on the dirty platforms, and in the mist of parting I soaked my handkerchief in benzine and sucked violently. The face of my grandma flashed past my mind's eye with Johannesburg's neon lights. The wheels spoke to me and I replied. Why my father and granny had told me I would become a man did not concern me then for my head was spinning. The ticket bearing my name and destination was attached to my coat. Sophiatown lay far, far behind. It had given me no hint of what I would encounter on my return to the City of Gold.

And as the wheels rattled and grunted on the tracks, the compartment twisted and turned violently — topsy-turvy; my head spun around one million times; zwing, zwang zwingeling. The benzine drew curtains over my eyes. I slipped into a deep, deep sleep.

Mr Joyce was waiting for me on Durban station. As I alighted he took my bags and ordered me to follow him. The ambulance-type van raced through the city streets without a word from Mr Joyce or me. I didn't like speaking English so I just stared at the passing lights. Suddenly he asked if I spoke English. *'Nie so goed nie'* (Not too well), I replied.

'It won't be long before you will be able to,' he said. 'St Theresa's is an English home.' I nodded, hoping he would stop.

'Do you speak any African languages?' asked Mr Joyce.

'Tswana, I speak Tswana well. My mother is a Tswana,' I added hesitantly, not sure that it was the right thing to say.

The vehicle came to a halt. Prayers had just ended and the boys and the nuns went their respective ways. I was led into a waiting-room in the convent and a stoutly built nun, Mother Charles, who was in charge of the institution, took both my hands in hers and said: 'So this is Donald, the boy who has come to us to be a man. We don't know if we can make you one, but we certainly are going to try.'

Her face was round and chubby, and her hands soft and warm. Her clothes were snow-white and spotlessly clean. A fresh crispness hung about her like newly washed and ironed sheets. There was a gold ring on her left third finger and I discovered later that she and the other nuns who lived at the convent were 'Brides of Jesus'. Mother Charles summoned another nun and told her to take me to the dining-room, and as I followed her, I noticed that an unearthly silence pervaded the premises. Nuns walked quietly with bowed heads, hands tucked into their long sleeves. They carried rosaries, crossed themselves and prayed softly. A statue of St Theresa, patron saint of the institution, watched quietly from the corner of the sitting-room. A bowl of fresh roses at the feet of the statue almost matched those she carried. Then a church bell struck the hour of six and, as if held in a spell, the nun in front of me and those we had passed in the long passage stopped dead in their tracks, made the sign of the cross and went down on their knees. It was the Angelus, which in the Roman Catholic faith marks the time of the Annunciation to the Virgin Mary by the Angel Gabriel, that she was to give birth to the child Jesus.

The garden in front of the convent building was neatly kept and the purple flowers on the thorny hedge were like a royal necklace. A tall spruce kept vigil, like some angelic sentinel guarding the convent against the forces of evil. There were also jacaranda trees near the church. The convent was on the same land as the home, at the top of Mayville, a suburb of Durban. It seemed most Catholics had to walk uphill to speak and commune with their Maker, because the church of St Theresa was on the highest point of the hill. There were only boys at the home, most of them orphans. The boarders or private pupils wore their own clothes, whereas the orphans wore khaki shirts and trousers. On Sundays the special blue shirt and navy blue trousers may have given the impression that the orphans were well-dressed, but it was not the case. Boarders, like myself, mostly wore good shoes and during the winter months it was painful to see barefooted boys with cracked heels and chapped lips and hands, braving the cold. It was not that the nuns didn't care, but the state subsidy did not provide cash for shoes.

St Theresa's home, where children would sometimes cry for a parent they had never seen or known, for a mother lost in childbed or a father who had run away. . . . Sometimes an unexpected visit from some almost-forgotten relative would transform the life of an orphan: the boy's face would light up like a sunrise, and he would rush eagerly to the visitors' parlour in the nuns' quarters. But there were also times of aloneness when we would go to the washroom verandah and sing our songs of longing and sadness:

> *It was a cold winter's night*
> *That my poor mother died*
> *And I stood by her bedside*
> *Until the last moment came*
> *And she held me so kindly*
> *And she asked me to pray,*
> *Dear mother in heaven*
> *Look down upon your child. . . .*

But still I would like to think that the happiness exceeded the sad memories and the longing. The boys from the home were a special breed: tough, hardened and definitely more mature than the well-fed day-pupils. We arranged our own concerts and festivals with the help of the nuns and our supervisors, Mr Joyce and Mr Joubert-King. St Theresa's boys excelled in every kind of sport and were especially outstanding in the martial arts. This was to benefit me on my return to Sophiatown.

It was during the War years and food was scarce at the institution. We had massive appetites and those of us who had friends among the day-pupils used whatever money they gave us to buy extra food like beans and bread. Brown sugar baked in an old tin, to which we would add peanuts, produced our home-grown toffee called thumbs or tamalaykee. The older boys often sold the toffee in the dormitories at night after lights-out. The crunching sound as the boys bit into their brittle toffee was a sort of lullaby, a sweet way to end the day.

We often stole green avocado pears from the privately owned yards surrounding the home. We would wrap them in paper and bury them in a secret place for consumption at a later date. But the boys had a way of sniffing out food — like hungry dogs, so that when you returned to retrieve your pears, a gaping hole greeted you with disappointment. Stealing was second nature at the institution. Telling lies was also vital, because if you told the truth or confessed to a misdemeanour the resident priest or the male supervisors would see to it that you were severely punished. Punishment, they said, was the visible way of ensuring that an offender had repented. Some of us even lied when we were veritably caught with our hands in the cookie-jar. Lying became almost instinctive.

There were African and Indian boys, but among the coloured ones, some were so fair that they could easily have passed for white. These were the offspring of white and black, whose mothers did not want to risk embarrassment. And so the home was a dumping ground for children whom the nuns had to clean, care for and mould into good Catholic Christians.

The institution was officially built for coloured children, but Catholic policy was open and non-selective. Father Hugo, an eccentric French priest, helped to bring the light of Catholicism to the Protestant children. Although we were never forced to become Catholics, prayer became a way of life so that we lived Catholic, laughed, played, slept and even ate Catholic. Most of us had no choice but to become Catholics. And it was quite an experience for me to learn so profoundly the ways of God. I mastered the catechism and sang the Mass in Latin. But it was also painful — Father Hugo saw to that with his cat-o'-nine-tails. I thought he was a cruel man. There were times I really hated him. He had more time and love for his dogs which I had to clean and brush as one of my many chores than he had for us. I also looked after and milked his goats.

One day, after I had washed the four dogs, I took them for a walk which turned out to be my undoing: I was severely punished by Father Hugo for a near-mortal sin. The dogs and I, taking our first taste of freedom, dashed through the large procession yard, down the pawpaw, mango and banana groves, across the dirty stream and finally through the bramble bushes. What a sight the dogs were when we returned! Ten times the priest's whip lashed my backside until blood signalled him to halt the chastisement. My hatred of him found expression and I avenged myself by throwing lavatory disinfectant into his prized fish pond; I stole a bagful of his Sunday collection pennies, and opened some of his bird cages. Severe and more drastic punishment followed which included the shaving of my head in hot cross bun fashion. I was forced to wear sack-cloth and like a hypocritical Pharisee, atone for my sins. I was warned that I might be expelled from the institution. I became an object of scorn and from that moment on I became a fighter, taking on older and bigger boys, and earned the name Don Terror.

I saw and heard strange things at St Theresa's. Some boys kissed and cuddled each other and spoke of sex with the teachers. One of the older boys was expelled from the home together with a young coloured novice for having had an unholy relationship. Many of us knew that Cecil and the girl loved each other and that they met secretly in the shadows; we never informed on them. It was beautiful to us that one of our kind could find someone to love, especially a nun. For the nuns took the place of our mothers and fathers; they took the place of lovers.

Trouble always seemed to follow me. The supervisors and I never got on and life became unbearable for me.

When my grandmother died in 1946 the news of her death was kept from me, and it was only on my return to Johannesburg for the December holidays that I learned of the tragedy. I had wanted so much for her to see the man I had become — reading and writing, speaking English; even praying.

As I entered my grandpa's house accompanied by my cousin Koukie who had met me at the station, I felt an uncanny emptiness; something was missing from the house. My aunt Baby was busy at the stove and uncle Willie who was drinking beer just stared at me.

'Ma-Minnie's dead, Don.' My aunt's voice was subdued. 'And everything has gone wrong ever since.'

I didn't respond but walked through to my grandpa's room. Perhaps he could explain the emptiness, the detachment. The door was locked and I peeped through the keyhole. Red wine bottles stood at one end of the table and the old man was asleep.

I went back to the kitchen where Uncle Willie asked how I was and remarked that I'd grown fast.

'It was hell in the War,' he said suddenly, and lifted his shirt. There were deep scars on his side. He said part of his finger had been shot off at Alamein. Then as I put out my hand to touch the scars, he hit me full on the mouth. I fell out of the kitchen door against the grapevine. He cursed and walked away.

'Willie's gone mad. It happened just after Ma's death and he's blaming himself and the old man. You know how it is. Since Ma's death. . . .'

I walked to the tap. My mouth was cut and bleeding. I was angry. Hurt. My father was not home nor was the nurse I had left behind. I was lonely and longed to see my mother.

The death of my granny left a huge vacuum in my life and I remained with my father until the end of 1947, amid a fast changing world and a family that was disintegrating, but I was helpless to do anything about it.

. . . . For how does a child say to his elders: 'stop this thing or do that thing or else you may perish.'? How can a child stop a house or his family from falling apart when he has come home to nothing and no-one, when what joy and laughter he knew before his departure had been transformed into loneliness both deep and palpable?

I guess I didn't really understand what was going on. I didn't see much of my own parents. My grandpa was almost a stranger and often spoke about my grandma. About their lives; how they had met. How she had always obeyed him. He talked about his love for her and how there had been many other women, but he didn't choose any of them. During his youth beautiful white girls had thrown themselves at his feet, but he loved my granny. My grandpa would speak of her constant companionship and the strength she had given him during the lean years, after he jumped ship in Cape Town. How, when he was penniless and destitute, she gave him comfort and her body. Then, with the blessing of her parents, she followed him into the heart of Johannesburg — sharing the trials of a foreigner in a foreign country. They started a balloon-making business and when the old man went to work in the mines, she stayed home to watch the growing family. The move to Sophiatown gave promise of a life of plenty and security. But she worked as a midwife to augment their income. She was a woman known and loved by thousands, he said. And when she died, hundreds of people of all races had paid their last respects to her. Father Trevor Huddleston, an Anglican priest who was later to influence my troubled life, had conducted the funeral service.

As cities have landmarks of historical value and sentiment, so was my granny a landmark for Sophiatown. Many people have substantiated this, and deep inside of me I want to believe it. Whenever the old man spoke her name, tears fell from his semi-blind eyes; eyes that had seen the gold build the city of Johannesburg; eyes that were never to see his native Italy again; eyes that wept when he reminisced about his land and his people, their history of war and peace. How he had sung in the streets of Naples after he ran away from the strict discipline of his farming parents, especially his stern father Pasquale who had made him and his sisters work in the fields and gather crops and trample grapes. My grandpa often told of times when church bells sounded the Angelus; how he used to peep through his fingers to watch his father mumble the same, monotonous prayer, day in and day out. He left home to seek his fortune and finally landed in South Africa, where many generations of coloured offspring were to follow.

I had wasted the whole of 1947 in Sophiatown without any schooling and I longed to return to St Theresa's. There was nothing for me among my people. I saw very little of my father, who was trying at that time to pull the family together. I was told that he made a vow at my granny's deathbed never to touch liquor again and I watched him stick to his oath until his death. My mother paid occasional visits, but I felt a deep desire for the home. When I left for the institution in January 1948 only my cousin Koukie saw me off at the station. Forgotten was the bit about my going to become a man. That dream, it seemed, had died with my granny.

The train's wheels spun fast, and I thought about my cousin Chossie, who had been pampered and virtually raised in an eggshell. How I loved him and wished that he could also leave the accursed place. The sound of the wheels spinning on the tracks had always fascinated me. There was no benzine to lull me to sleep this time and I thought of my granny — why did she have to die?

Back at St Theresa's life appeared unchanged. The nuns and the boys were glad to see me. Soon after my return, Mother Charles died. It was one of the saddest things to happen at the home. We recited the rosary for days on end. Father Hugo prayed for the safekeeping of her soul and that God might remember her in paradise. I grew attached to the home and the enmity between Father Hugo and me dissolved. I was appointed group leader in charge of fifty other

boys. The best years of my life were spent at St Theresa's and I longed to prove to my folks that I was going to be the man my granny
had wanted me to become. I learned the manners of please and thank
you; of dressing and speaking properly, but my disposition was no
different to that of the other boys at the home because my family's
indifference had seemingly relegated me to orphanhood. I got hardly
any mail from either of my parents, and the occasional food or gift
parcels from my grandpa stopped coming. But for the memory of
my granny, everyone and everything receded from my mind.

I absorbed whatever came my way with a deep hunger to excel in
whatever I did. I spoke quietly and believed that my stay at the home
was the will of God and that Father Hugo, however cruel he seemed
to be, was a disciple of God's work on earth.

The loneliest times for me at the boarding school were during the
Christmas holidays when my folks forgot to send my train fare home.
Well that was what I told the other boys when they asked me why my
rich Italian family had not posted me the money. The luckier boarders
teased and mocked us as they prepared for their various destinations.

Christmas time brought with it immense joy for some and the pain
of aloneness for others. And amid the cheering and jeering as the
home's Black Maria — always driven by Mr Joyce — hooted
incessantly on its way out of the yard, I would feel a lump of envious
pain in my throat. Envy that they were going home to their families;
pain that I would be remaining behind; the sum total of which showed on the faces of the children who were 'complete' orphans — complete meant having no known living relations.

. . . Are there really such people in this world? Could there be
complete orphans when the priest and nuns told us that we were all
one family in Christ — children of the One Living God who had
made heaven and earth? When each one was the other's keeper? This
said, could there still be complete orphans? And how was it that I,
who had parents and a rich family in the place that is called
Johannesburg, could feel so orphaned, so forgotten?

The Black Maria zoomed out of sight taking my heart with it and
leaving behind an empty shell in dirty khaki clothes.

The other boys remaining would run excitedly behind the vehicle
waving and calling to their departing friends. I would walk quietly
away past the dormitories, down the steps near the dinner hall which

was just above the washing and showering bay. Below it lay the uneven sports ground and the iron-roofed sheds where we used to play and fight, and share the spoils of sweet potatoes and milk we had stolen from Livingstone's yard — a white-owned farm near the home. Farther down was a dirty stream that ran for miles. Once over the thick steel pipe that stretched across the stream onto an area of guava and avocado trees, I would not turn to look back on my tracks. Instead I would climb the hillock and make my own path towards the cemetery to sit and gaze at the speeding motor vehicles.

A cemetery is not only a place for the burial of the dead. Thoughts too have to be killed; to be wrapped in black calico and rivetted in a steel coffin, and then consigned to the earth. But my thoughts, like my pain, refused to die naturally or be killed. And so I sat on the huge warm stones and stared at the vehicles crawling along and the lizards that shot past my gaze like four-legged shooting stars. The warm and humid December sun filled the atmosphere with a strange, tangible heat that gave me comfort in a place of death. And longing and loneliness visited me and took their places beside me on the stone. I ached to have wings; strong, powerful wings that could lift me high above the cemetery; above the Catholic convent school they called a home; up, up, to the fluffy grey-white clouds that scarcely moved. I ached to have wings to carry me home to people I knew and loved and was trying to understand; to places I could quickly relate to and find in them a genuine sense of belonging — an anchor for my fears and my loneliness at Christmas. Then voices deep in me would speak the language we spoke at 16 Gerty Street, Sophiatown in Johannesburg; inside our house and outside in the streets that would one day claim me for their own.

I could not really belong to Durban. It could never be home to me — no matter what the priest and nuns told us at the time.

I had mixed feelings about remaining at the institution, but a state welfare decree forced the issue: the Catholic authorities were to stop catering for private boarders like myself. The home, we were told, would become an orphanage, because younger boys with more urgent welfare needs were going to take our places. Something that would always live in my mind was the sight of new arrivals weeping as they jumped out of the government vehicle to begin their lives at the institution. They cried when they came; I cried when I left the home.

I arrived at Johannesburg station in the company of the Dukhi brothers Rishi and Vinai. There was no-one to meet me; no hearty welcome, no garlands. . . . It was the end of 1949.

My tin suitcase was heavy. Vinai and Rishi, who like me had been affected by the orphans only ruling at St Theresa's, walked with me from the station to the bus terminus. They alighted at Vrededorp — the hometown of the renowned self-exiled South African writer Peter Abrahams — and promised that we would meet again.

Johannesburg had not changed much. The Indian shops and street vendors were still part of the scene. I got off in Good Street, Sophiatown's most notorious and populous street.

No-one expected me, although I knew that the sisters had sent a telegram informing my father that I was coming home. I was not excited either, and walked casually into my grandpa's kitchen. All was quiet. I entered the main bedroom and there, as on my 1946 return, I saw my grandpa sleeping soundly, his head embedded in a mound of cushions. Heavy snoring came from his cigar-stained mouth. I went to my aunt Baby's house, but neither she, her husband Albert nor my cousin Chossie was home. I went to my father's. The sound of a baby crying caught my ears, a sound I loved and had grown accustomed to at the institution. On the bed, completely naked, lay a chubby baby boy. A tall coffee-coloured woman, beautiful and big-eyed, greeted me by my name. She said the child was called Pasquale — Pashie for short — and I instantly loved him. Rebecca was my father's new 'wife' and Pashie's mother. The nurse had obviously been sacked, like so many women I had known before.

I greeted Rebecca with some trepidation and didn't wait to continue the conversation. I thought of my mother. Why wasn't she there in the house where the new wife moved about so authoritatively? Why had there not been somebody to meet me at the station?

A sudden anger drove me blindly from my 'stepmother' and I went to an adjoining room where my uncle Goon and his wife Lizzie lived. They, too, were not legally husband and wife but I loved them and found them sympathetic and understanding. Twin little boys crawled about noisily on the unwashed wooden floor. On a crooked bed and slumped clumsily over the side, lay my uncle. Next to him was a jam tin with the remains of a home-made liquor concoction called Barberton, which is made from kaffir-corn, yeast, brown sugar and brown bread, all mixed in a large tin filled with water and left to stand overnight. The yeast is usually packed in for a harder kick and in some circles the concoction was called kill-me-quick. All my uncles drank Barberton and when they didn't eat well, they contracted liquor-flame, a disease that affects the skin, so that one can actually peel it off. Those who had liquor-flame often wore long sleeved garments to hide the peeling.

My uncle's red eyes stared blankly at me for a while and he muttered in Afrikaans, 'Don, where were you all the time?'

I laughed quietly and picked up one of the twins. God, they were identical! And restless! The other twin tugged at my leg and I lifted him into my other arm. Just then my aunt Lizzie, a battle-scarred, buxom African woman and former convict — who at one time had been a wardress in a mental home — entered the room. She was tough and yet a kind and loving woman.

'*Haai*, Don. Is it really you? God how you've grown! Just look at you. Who would say it was that small Don of yesterday?' For an African her Afrikaans was good. She kissed me full on the mouth and the smell of alcohol on her breath told me I was home. 'The one on your right is Kenneth. No, Raymond. Dammit, these twins are giving me a headache,' Lizzie cursed. She asked how I was and how I liked my stepmother. She said that my mother had once visited them and the stepmother had been rude to her. God my mother! No one should dare touch my mother! Then turning to her man she said, almost indifferently, 'Goon's been drunk for days, weeks, months on end, Don. He just drinks and drinks. Like he's the one that's got all the problems.' Her lips were swollen and I guessed it had been another one of those beatings.

'Everything's gone wrong since Ma's death. Your grandpa has changed and is a bitter man. Danny and Willie have not completely overcome the strain of madness. Your uncle Danny has been in and out of Sterkfontein Mental Hospital.' Her voice had suddenly deepened. She may have remembered her days as a matron in a ward for insane women. She must have understood the torture of madness. 'Since Ma's death. . . .' But before she could finish her sentence I interrupted and told her to stop telling me about my granny's death.

'Don, stay with us. Don't go and live with your father, you will be very unhappy.'

It was the assurance I needed, so I made up my mind not to live with my father, come what might. The yard was quiet save for the barking of our dogs. Rover was old and Baardbek (bearded mouth), the once cheeky terrier, was quiet and subdued. In another kennel lay Bruno, a dog I had instantly developed a dislike for. 'Keep away from that dog,' warned my grandpa's house worker, Old Tom Isaacs, who had been with the family for as long as I could remember. 'That Bruno has bitten the *oubaas* several times. Once it jumped for his neck and if I hadn't been there, your grandfather would have followed the *oumies,*' (old missus) my granny. His age-ing face with its strong Indian features contorted into a grimace.

I did not accept my aunt Lizzie's offer to live with her because of lack of space. My uncle Frank also lived with his common-law wife Patience in the same room. So I moved in with my cousin Koukie who lived in one of my grandpa's spare rooms.

Koukie and I used to talk long into the night about almost everything under the sun. He had been a brilliant student, but found it hard to live with his parents. It was not long before I followed in his path of rebellion. The environment was the complete opposite of the Catholic school. There were more people in Sophiatown than before I had left and everything was strange and hostile, even my old friends had changed and it took a lot of adjusting to get acquainted with boys in the neighbourhood. I spoke differently and even my Afrikaans was almost highbrow. The slang too had changed and everybody was playing tough-guy. It was not long before I was in-volved in many fights, so that street-fighting became second nature to me. My boxing ability and guts won me a following that became one of Sophiatown's most dreaded 'child' gangs called the Vultures.

The halo of good Catholic upbringing fell and gave way to the horns of rebellion and violence. . . .

And so I came back to the cruel, fascinating world of Sophiatown which would reclaim me as it had so many other young boys and girls. All the strict discipline and Catholic upbringing would be nullified and I would be returned to the bosom of my 'mother', Sophiatown. For she was in me, and I was in the warmth and com-fort of her dirty blood. Many had tried to break their umbilical cord but only a few had managed to escape and transcend her legacy.

Sophiatown throbbed and heaved like a nymph craving love, drawing me ever deeper and closer to her body from where I heard the laughter and cries of a people bound and shackled by the ancient monster called fear; where I watched my own family fall to pieces; where men and women — politicians and policemen, priests and sinners — loved and hated with such intensity that I believed God, the Catholic God I knew and feared, had forsaken Sophiatown, and had forsaken and cursed my family.

4. Sophiatown

*N*obody can write the real story of Sophiatown, the rise and fall of the township, the magic and wonderment of the place. . . . It was inhabited by an estimated 200 000 people of different ethnic backgrounds who lived tightly-knit, mixing cultures, traditions and superstitions in a manner perhaps unique in Southern Africa. Every conceivable space was occupied by a living thing — man or animal.

It was a place where the poor were victims of subtle exploitation at the hands of shrewd Chinese, Indian, white and in a few instances, African businessmen, who drained the masses very discreetly. Food was sold in small quantities but at huge profits. A five-penny loaf of bread would be sliced into twelve or fifteen pieces and sold at a penny a slice. Other commodities such as cooking oil, sugar, maize-meal, tea and candles were neatly packed into three-penny or five-penny parcels which realised bigger profits. And the unsuspecting customers paid, unaware that they were victims of bloodsucking. Even house rentals were paid on an instalment basis. Property-owners, especially the Jews and Indians, built several single quarters on small plots and also encouraged the erection of wood and zinc shanties at rentals of two and three pounds a month. Most of the yards had a single lavatory and one tap which were shared by 150 to 200 residents. People and the township dogs relieved themselves against the same walls and put their mouths under the same taps. Beneath the same tree they had their brief sexual encounters.

The yards were small and stinking wherever people lived in this crowded communal way. And you would find a man or woman lying drunk in the grime and slime and debris, breathing the foul air of a dispossessed and forsaken life — men and women robbed of those vital fibres that divide man from beast.

There were times of searching for a loved one in some alley; finding him or her wounded in a hospital or jail, or dead in a morgue. Or checking for a husband or father, a brother or a son who had never returned home from work. Or waiting for a mother, an aunt or sister who did not get off the bus or tram where you usually waited for them. Then the anguish and anxiety that would follow reports of a woman raped, beaten and robbed by the jobless and won't-work brigades of *tsotsis* who owned the days and ruled the nights. This was Sophiatown, the Kofifi of the *majietas* (city slickers) and of the *moegoes* or *bar-rees* (greenhorns). Life there was interestingly challenging and dangerous.

Sophiatown, the city of many faces: kind, cruel, pagan, Christian, Islamic, Buddhist and Hindu, and the face of what was called Law and what was made Criminal. Each face told its own story; held its own secrets and added to the book that was Kofifi — the little Chicago of Johannesburg.

The Face of Joy was vividly portrayed on Guy Fawkes night and Christmas Day by children from all cultural backgrounds as well as many adults with young hearts. Everyone looked forward to those days because of the spirit of festivity and the carnival atmosphere that generated from among the township dwellers. It was a captivating show of bedazzlement and colour and comedy; many people hardly aware at the time of the political significance of Guy

Fawkes Day. Paint, polish and powder were prettily plastered on young faces as the children enacted in impromptu pantomimes their parents' roles. People of diverse ethnic groupings danced together, ate and drank and loved each other in a spirit of togetherness and understanding. And I was among them, kissing mouths that smelled of white man's liquor and other concoctions; singing and dancing for a penny or two. Christmas brought a cleanliness with it that was both physical and spiritual. Families who hardly knew the Christian faith suddenly remembered its Founder in fervent prayer, in beauty and in revelry; lifting those who were downtrodden and outcast. Enemies shook hands and good friends consolidated their friendship with gifts and wishes, and new commitments to love.

This was Sophiatown.

Christmas was that period when tables sank under the weight of delicious foods. Open generosity abounded among all the people as families marched to their traditional places of worship to pray to the Saviour they had so long forgotten; the God they hardly knew; the God who, some said, had forsaken them. This day of all other days the Babe would welcome them; this day of all other days they would be united with the Babe in their sordid surroundings and poverty. This day of all other days at least, they would be cleansed and purified of all sin and shame.

It was also a time when they could drink themselves to oblivion without having to fear arrest for drunkenness or for having walked in a white suburb late at night without the official permit of police approval. *'Heppie, my baas,'* they would shout; 'for this day at least, *heppie, my baas. . . .'* and the *baas* in his policeman's tunic would nod approvingly and rise magnanimously to the spirit of the occasion: *'Ja jong'* (yes boy) drink yourself to pieces for when Boxing Day has ended, you shall see me again in all my glory and power. *Ja heppie,* my boy. . . .'

Christmas Day relieved some of the tensions the people experienced the whole year round, so that those who had grudges and scores to settle would postpone them to a later date. As a child, I loved this most exciting and uplifting time of the year. We were lavished with presents and money by our relatives and even perfect strangers. *Heppie* was the password that evoked spontaneous generosity, a genuineness of spirit and open displays of love.

Sadness brought us together too. People would gather at the home of the bereaved to offer comfort and condolences: a packet of sugar, candles, soap, food and anything that would by way of compassion reach out to lift the burden of sorrow. There would always be the blanketed old woman bringing her bundle of sympathy to show that she was aware (as the African saying goes) that misfortune walks in the queue; tomorrow it might be her turn in the shadow of death or in the misfortune of arrest, or one of those many troubles that befall people in a land where great wealth was shared among the chosen few; a land whose laws were geared for the systematic destruction of millions who were not of the chosen.

Yet Christmas brought them together in a spirit of charity. Children who had not known a real meal all year round were given as much as they could eat. And the man and woman who hid and ran from those who represented the law would find a moment of respite to drink and walk without fear of arrest. Small mercies in a land of great Christian values; small but welcome nonetheless.

'Heppie, my baas; for this day at least, *heppie, my baas. . . .'*

Then there was the Law. A grim, ugly face, distorted by ruthlessness and corruption. Not all the laws of the statute book, for there are eternally valid statutes; laws carried down from the father's father; laws to protect, defend and give respectability to society. But some that were unique to South Africa, and the representation of them called the Police. A representation that had to execute and uphold the edifices of the Whole of the Law. Yet it was forged with deep mistrust, brutality, threat and abuse. It did not matter whether you were law-abiding or criminal; everybody was victim to its viciousness; the extortion racket which allowed lawbreakers immunity from arrest, the bribery and corruption of high-ranking policemen, which dictated a way of life.

This was that part called the Police.

The cells were packed with African offenders, the courts convicting them in routine fashion — accused of being in a white area at night, while white people were asleep. In the daytime it was all right: African women were 'girls' and the men 'garden boys'.

At night the African men would be treated as lurking menaces out for the blood of the white man, or rapists to brutalise the sanctity of white women. Not because they were women; mostly because they were white. Black women arrested for not having the night pass special were taken for rides to lonely spots by black and white policemen for sex in exchange for release. It was also common to see African men being grabbed by their trousers in full view of their wives and children and ordered to produce their passes. Failure to produce your pass meant terms of up to six months in jail or being commandeered to work on some Afrikaner's farm at the cheapest rate of remuneration — not more than two shillings a day. Sometimes the 'offenders' retaliated because of the humiliating manner in which these documents were demanded. I saw many dead policemen, victims of crowds angered by these officers' callous disregard for human dignity. There were some good ones, but because they wore a common badge, they were all equally loathed. Children would often spit when the police passed on their usual raids for dagga or the illegal sale of the white man's liquor or home-made concoctions. The women paid us to keep watch for the police trucks known as *kwela-kwela* — which is Zulu for 'ride-ride'.

'Zinja!' (Dogs!) we would shout, so that the entire neighbourhood echoed our warning cries, which gave the illegal traders time to hide their wares. The police knew every trick we contrived because of their many informers. The concoctions were hidden in huge holes under piles of ash and dirt heaps. The police would jab long iron spikes into the ground until the drums were detected, unearthed and their contents spilled out into the yard. No-one could be arrested for such finds. In fact these hiding places were deliberately chosen by the brewers: what is in the ground belongs to the ground. The police knew this and were often seen pointing threateningly at the women in the yards. But we knew there were some holes that were never poked at or looked for; holes whose owners had paid the usual protection fee, lubricating the palms of hard-up Boers and their black lackeys. Even senior officers were guilty of taking bribes or extorting money from Chinese, Indian and African businessmen who traded illegally. Young boys were beaten when they were caught sounding their 'Dogs are here' warning, because it meant a loss of revenue. The beatings were often so severe that a firm and bitter hatred of the police was born inside of them — and inside of me.

. . . These are the men that my father hates. The ones who shot my brother when he tried to run away because his pass was not in order. And the black ones who pimp and sell out on their own people then smile at the Boers when they grab my sister by her breast. *'Lekker swart vleis, my basie'* (Nice black meat, my *baas*). And how the black ones laughed when the Boers pulled the blanket off my father's bed and shone their torches on my mother's naked body. And the look on father's face and the clenching of his teeth in useless anger and fear; his manhood diminished in front of his woman. These are the men. . . .

We were shooting dice on the sand pavement near Ah Poen Leong's Supply Store in Gerty Street, Sophiatown. He passed right through, almost as if we were invisible, bumping me aside, the money in my hand falling into the sand. I swore and cursed, looking up at him: 'Hey, what the bloody hell!' But his eyes penetrated my skull, and I tried to re-circulate my blood frozen by his gaze. He said something that sounded like *kap-kwai*, which I later discovered to be the Chinese equivalent for 'kaffir'. He mumbled another weird, incomprehensible syllable, and with a sharp turn, hopped into Ah Poen's shop, and then suddenly turned around to wave his finger at me: 'You *kap-kwai!*' My friends, and some older people who had been watching, burst out laughing at Dai-Sok, as he was known in our street — a street where women outnumbered the menfolk by four to one. Into this long street came Dai-Sok, walking straight out of an American cowboy movie in which he might have played the part of a fastidious Chinese cook.

He wore a black silken suit complete with matching cap and slippers, but minus the traditional pigtail. His yellow face was rough and scraggy, with countless deep rivulets of wrinkles that criss-crossed in all directions, even eastwards, from where Dai-Sok's ship must have set sail for South Africa, the new frontier of milk and honey. Dirty, tobacco-stained, racoon teeth jutted out of his small mouth like uninvited guests. Some bad boys even teased that his teeth had been specially shaped for human flesh, creating a fear of all Chinese among the younger children. Only four and a half feet high, Dai-Sok appeared taller at first glance, probably because the pipes of his trousers stopped way above his ankles, as if to indicate that he was growing every day.

His hands were small and delicate, with a sensitivity and gentleness found usually in convents and monasteries. Dai-Sok's eyes had a certain warmth about them, telling you he had seen much in his days; eyes that seemed to understand the hidden meanings of life and death. But he cleverly masked that wisdom under the crust of an abrupt and obstreperous demeanour, so that most of the kids in our neighbourhood developed a deep fear for him.

The tiny bits of English Dai-Sok ventured to speak only compounded the problem of communication, so much so that people would actually stop dead in their tracks when he spoke. It was a strange mixture of gibberish and Oriental pidgin, spluttering at jet-speed from his beautiful thin lips.

I often tried, perhaps out of a silly sense of bravado, to reach out and break the sheath of icy mystery that hung around him, but to no avail.

'Don Zinga,' said Stretch one day, 'why are you always trying so hard to make friends with that stupid gong?' Gong was a common derogatory term used in the townships for the Chinese. I did not answer, but he continued probing: 'It's not like you to play soft, bra; let's give him some of our black magic, and who knows we might even break him.'

I nodded. It *was* time we changed our tactics.

Dai-Sok picked up a few English and Afrikaans words, as well as some phrases of Sophiatown *tsotsi taal,* and before long, he began operating a game of chance called *koppie* dice, played with three dice and a board numbered one to six. The dice would be covered by a cup, and Dai-Sok would rattle them while the bets were being placed. When he lifted the cup he would pay those who had correctly selected the numbers which came up on the dice. The bets increased on Fridays, and he would make a substantial profit on those days.

One Friday I instructed one of my gang members to turn off the lights, and substituted a pair of loaded dice that always called up numbers five and six. We cleaned Dai-Sok out. Hot curses of *kap-kwai!* reverberated through the shop, and I watched with helpless anxiety as the infuriated Chinese smashed the dice with a hammer, collected the pieces and flung them in my face. The mercury from the loaded dice shone on my cheeks.

'You blettee *kap-kwai*, you tingkee me tom — stupid. You hum-bokkee — cheat Dai-Sokkee weetee lopanee — robbing — dicee. You come backee, I killee you, you blettee *kap-kwai.* . . .'

That was the end of our gambling itch. If we dared go near the shop, Dai-Sok would dash inside and come out brandishing an ugly butcher's chopper. We became the laughing stock of Gerty Street, to the open delight of our persecutor. But we planned our vengeance. Dai-Sok had no wife, and our street was a veritable saucy harem. We knew that Dai-Sok paid good money for a night of sex; and there was no *kap-kwai* when it came to that. 'Stretch, my bra — my brother, it's time we really taught that gong some manners,' I said. Stretch nodded: '*Ja*, let's put him in his place once and for all.'

I instructed him to dress up like some floozy: make-up, jewellery, high-heeled shoes, and turban — complete with matching handbag swinging from his hip. We laughed and giggled at our diabolical conspiracy, rehearsing like actors for the opening night. Excitement and expectation ripped down my back as I watched Stretch go through his act of deception.

And the moon, an unwilling accomplice, hid her face behind a long, thick cloud. Vengeance would be shared, whether she liked it or not. . . .

Dai-Sok waited like a bird of prey for the arrival of *any* illicit lover. So vividly was Stretch's buttocks defined by his sister's dress that when he sauntered past the sex-crazed Chinese, we whistled and made naughty catcalls. The big white earrings danced like two bright stars above the white pearl necklace that rested on Stretch's home-made breasts. Our boy was a dazzling spectacle of seductive beauty, which could well have attracted other hungry suitors. A bottle of Cologne splashed on his outfit, Stretch brushed appetisingly past Dai-Sok, who instinctively stroked the boy's backside.

'Oh, Dai-Sokkee,' giggled our shy 'sister'. 'What you want?'

'You wantee cockee; I give monee! You want me daaling you cockee?' Dai-Sok replied so rapidly, so very ardently, that I actually pitied him, I nearly burst out screaming. Stretch did not reply. Instead he confidently flung his buttocks to the left and to the right, and shot out his long, bangled arm, opened his hand, and said: 'Yessee, I wantee, but first givee me five pound,' the shrill voice suddenly becoming a hoarse croak.

The game's up, I told myself; dammit our game's up. . . . Then in an instant, as if he read my thoughts, Stretch calmly said: 'Me wantee, but first you givee money, my sweetee lovee daaling.' Dai-Sok melted. He put some notes into our hero's hand.

'Takee off your tlouzaa (trousers),' the sweet smelling Stretch said. 'Now me wantee cockee.' The Chinaman's pants fell meekly below his knees to reveal his manhood, erect and ready. Stretch, who had no panties on, obediently lifted his dress. Dai-Sok placed his bony fingers under the dress to feel his partner and gave a loud, shattering scream that shook me.

'You blettee *kap-kwai!* bastaa! (bastard) I killee you chop-chop!' He tried to run but fell on his hands screaming, *'Kap-kwai! Kap-kwai!'*

'You likee boss Dai-Sokkee,' teased Stretch, once more lifting his dress, exposing his backside. Our hero shook his hips to and fro and then dashed towards us laughing.

We had scattered in different directions, splitting our sides with hysterical and uncontrollable laughter. Onlookers joined in the fun as the man from China stomped and jumped about the street cursing Oriental expletives.

Vengeance had been not only sweet, but also profitable.

And tease Dai-Sok we did, with a satirical ditty resulting from his abortive sex drama. The song became a household tune throughout Sophiatown and other cosmopolitan townships of Johannesburg where Chinese people lived, loved and traded:

> *Ching-ga Mao le*
> *Taai bossee*
> *One sigalet*
> *And two toffee*

Yes, Ching the Chinaman was a tough boss, he got one cigarette and two toffees for his sexual lust. Dai-Sok and every other person of Chinese origin hated the tune, and reacted violently whenever they were teased. The others, of course, had not felt Dai-Sok's humiliation on the night of our delinquent merriment. And the hurt showed deep in his eyes. But he was not beaten. Vengeance would be his.

. . .Vengeance is an echo that comes back to us from the valley of our deeds, reminding us always that nobody wins in the game of retribution; that each is diminished by the pain of the other; that each is 'a part of the main'. But what of the child who, like his people, has never been taught or told of the finer human qualities of forgiveness, nor of the hurt of humiliation.

Long after our sex joke, amid signs of an unspoken truce, Dai-Sok calmly lured Stretch and me into the shop.

'Ton (Don), you come hepee (help) me in shoppee. I givee two pounds, stloo Got (strue's God) for one smo joppee (small job). You come?'

His voice was soft and pleading. We readily agreed, entering the shop through a side door.

'I wantee you washee taboo (shop counter). It velly dertee. You lookee taboo, you see how dertee,' Dai-Sok said, sinking to demonstrate how we should view the counter.

Stretch and I stooped to counter level.

'Velly dertee, you lookee!'

We held our positions, nodding sheepishly, and Dai-Sok blew violently into our eyes the red layer of chilli-pepper he had sprinkled onto the counter. Blinded, and groping helplessly, we screamed and cried and called our mothers. Dai-Sok's laughter was accompanied by heavy whip-lashes that opened cuts on my body and across my head. Stretch was screaming: 'Please, boss Dai-Sok, please don't hit my peepee! Don't hurt my peepee!' The whip stung me so violently, I urinated in my pants.

'You likee cockee, I hittee cockee, *kap-kwai!*' the Chinese jeered amid raucous outbursts of sarcastic laughter. I cannot to this day tell how Stretch and I managed to open the heavily bolted door and escape into the street in which we had hurt and humiliated Dai-Sok. After that Stretch hardly visited me nor did I ever venture to go near Ah Poen's shop. Other children in the neighbourhood also developed a new respect for the little Chinese, and their fear of him was increased.

Dai-Sok and many of his people quickly learned the ways of survival in the sprawling, politically doomed Sophiatown. They became part of its history, part of its cosmopolitan glory, part of its pain.

And when the government demolition squads came into our township, into our beautiful street, into our lives, none was left unscathed. The bulldozers came, saw, and assaulted every tin and wooden shack, every stately house and every shop. We were scattered like chaff.

Ah Poen Leong's Supply Store and gambling den crumbled alongside the houses. Ah Poen and his family trekked to a white suburb in Johannesburg, because the law conferred a white status on the Chinese in the land. Dai-Sok did not accompany the Ah Poens. He chose to remain in Sophiatown, finding work at another Chinese-owned store deep in the heart of the township. But the apartheid bulldozers offered him and countless other families no respite. They crushed and butchered every brick and plank and zinc structure. Everything. Everyone.

Africans, coloureds, Indians and even the non-political and

tightly-welded Chinese, reeled submissively before the iron monsters. None was spared, and our street — with its beautiful and ugly people, its shrubs and greenery, its pavements with pine and oak trees — died, murdered in the October of 1958, when the houses of the few more stubborn property-owners breathed their last. My family remained to witness the killings of other homes.

During those gruesome assaults Dai-Sok vanished. And it was only in the autumn of 1980, after twenty-two years, that I saw him again. On a park bench, near the Johannesburg library chewing on a piece of sandwich. He was old and haggard and dusty, with long unkempt hair that fell like crawling plants over his bent and broken shoulders. I called his name several times, each time louder, but got no response. Then, much closer to his ear, I said: 'Dai-Sokkee; it is me Ton. You remember me? *Kap-kwai?* Ah Poen's shop in Gerty Street, Sophiatown?' But I got no response. It seemed fruitless to go on trying. And as I raised my head, I saw scrutinous, suspicious eyes all around, seeming to undress me with their curiosity.

Then, as if to vindicate me before the strange and ignorant accusers, Dai-Sok lifted his head so slowly, it appeared a lifetime before he looked at me. A sudden, swift gush of wind whipped the trees, and a few autumn leaves blew between our gazes. How many autumns had it been since that day when a spritely Dai-Sok had hopped full of vigour into Ah Poen's shop?

. . . Men are like leaves. Now fresh and green with the strength and vigour of youth. Voluptuous leaves to adorn and clothe the tree of life, that others may find the support and comfort of shade. Shade from the blistering heat of the passion and anger of human cruelty. Men are like leaves: now the beauty and the zeal; now the change and decay and the slow dive to the waiting earth where all is equal. Then the burial. The oblivion. Men are like leaves. . . .

Dai-Sok peered cautiously from the corners of his narrow, bloodshot eyes, and nodded several times, slowly. Then he said, 'You, you *kap-kwai* you. . .' a smile crossing his face. At last the final truce; at last the long-sought, long-awaited crack in the human armoury, acknowledged at last in the twilight of his years. But as his head had come up, so too had it drooped, like a tired flower; like a heavy coffin sliding downward, taking with it all joy and laughter and all the unspeakable pain of loneliness.

I had many brushes with the police. Like the time I alighted from a train at the Nancefield railway station on a visit to my mother in White City Jabavu in what is today known as Soweto. A tall black policeman stopped me. His huge hands gripped my belt, pulling my trousers against my private parts.

'Pass!' he shouted, so that the passersby heard him.

'I'm a coloured,' I answered, using the password to a semblance of privilege and temporary safety and immunity. It would work now, as it had several times before when police raided our house in Sophiatown in their hunt for pass offenders.

'Half-caste *Boesman* is what you mean,' he said, tightening his lethal grip, so that my testicles moved into my bladder. Aware of his brute force, he pressed harder and harder, grinning sadistically. Urine ran down my thigh, wetting his hand. A blow stunned my jaw. Half-blinded, I sagged and his grip loosened. As I was coming to, another blow crushed into my ribs. Darkness. When I looked up there was a Boer policeman poking his baton at my exposed testicles.

'Wat's verkeerd, bruin balas?' (What's wrong, brown balls?) I tried to speak but he ordered me to get up and leave. I turned to his black colleague and promised I would get him someday.

'Get your kaffir-mother, you sonofabitch!' he shouted to attract the attention of the bystanders. Some people laughed. A woman tried to help but I recoiled from her, angered by their derisive looks and their laughter.

All my mother said when I told her of the incident was that I was beginning to understand one form of humiliation that was a way of life for her people.

'Now you know a bit. With coloureds it is different. You have many rights and privileges. Your colour ensures for you status and a future. No pass, no permits, no influx control, but it's bad when your skin is black. I'm happier now that I gave you to your father's people — otherwise you too would have suffered,' she told me without pity.

I argued that the policeman had been an African, a black person, and yet he had beaten me without regard for my youth. She replied that he had stopped being an African when he put on a police badge. He had become something totally different; a tool; a robot. Something else, but not an African. She said being an African was something great; transcending and human, with an open heart. In retrospect, she gave me something better than pity, for she helped me to believe in and understand Africanness. I wanted more than anything to be a true African.

In 1952 I was sixteen years old and would be seventeen in December. The winter was harsh and cold. I had already alienated myself from my father and most of the family at 16 Gerty Street; going astray — a street-fighter and thug for whom violence and obstinacy were the golden rule in the game of self-preservation. My folks didn't care, I didn't care and society cared least of all. My uncle Willie, the former World War II soldier, who was said at the time to be suffering from shell-shock, became openly and violently hostile towards me. His were the fists that had cut my lips on the first day of my return from the Catholic convent school in Durban. It had been his way of welcoming me back.

My grandfather had locked and bolted his house against me after it was discovered that I used to leave and re-enter it through one of the back windows. Burglaries had become common and frequently violent, and I was accused of having endangered his life. So another of so many doors had closed on me — some never to open again. Heavy steel doors of human indifference locking me out, isolating me, the same way I had rejected my family and shut them out.

One night I led the Vultures against the Styles gang at their haunt on the corner of Edward Road and Gold Street. It was a fierce, toe-to-toe encounter with no quarter given on either side. Knives penetrated into soft dark flesh. Axes, swords and tomahawks — crudely manufactured at home or newly-purchased from the hardware stores — crushed into bone and skull. Uncle Willie's army bayonet cracked with its jagged edge into Mkhuba's head. He turned around to stare at me in disbelief and terror as his blood spurted into my face and onto my clothes. He screamed. He ran. He fell. It was the end of the Styles gang.

The journey home was one of misguided triumph and song. Bloodied hands. Bloodied clothes. Bloodied and broken lives. but no matter. People would talk about us in the streets of Sophiatown, for that was what we lived for — to be noticed, to be spoken of and to be feared. Respect had nothing to do with it.

Others would look at us and cower — and even run away. But some would spit defiantly and challenge us to defend the brief, frail glory and all the infamy we had recklessly and foolishly won. But many more would salute us and even pat us on the back in praise for the flesh ripped apart, the bones crushed, and the life taken. Nothing more. Nothing less.

No-one cared.

My uncle found me asleep on my grandpa's verandah, wrapped in two dirty blankets I had bought with some shopkeeper's protection fee. His boot sagged into me and robbed my lungs of the cool pre-dawn air.

'Where the fucking hell's my bayonet? What did you do with it? Kill another miserable sonofabitch? Where's my weapon dammit?'

He was angry and mad for I had taken his war memento, his trophy, his only reward for having fought against the Nazis. He had fought and been wounded, returned home unsung and forgotten, and watched in silent envy while the white veteran soldiers were decorated and recompensed for their valour in facing the enemy — an enemy no different from the one who would someday give the order to destroy our home. I gave him the bayonet and he chased after me, his shouts epitomising graphically the state of my confused and rejected existence.

'Come here, you little bastard! Come let me end your fucking misery. . . .'

I laughed as we ran round the house. Two lost souls, two lost soldiers, each with a lost cause. I ducked and dodged, unconcerned and unmoved by the ferocity of his words.

That winter I contracted meningitis from sleeping on the cold cement verandah. It was the only time I really knew my folks — when they gathered round my hospital bed. It felt good and reassuring to see them rallying round me, however temporarily. As soon as I was 'out of danger' they lost interest.

The misery remained.

5. *Dumazile*

*W*oodwork class had ended late one Thursday in the month of September 1953. A soft, persistent rain drenched my head and shoulders and rolled down my neck. September Badenhorst pulled at my shirt.

'Let's run, Zinga,' he said, using a nickname my father had given to me. 'Come on,' he urged as I jerked from his grip.

'You know I love the rain,' was my response as I opened my mouth to catch the spray.

'You're mad. I'm running, I'm running.' His words still hung in the damp air as I watched him vanish around Mukkadam's butchery.

September was a tall, dark-skinned Sophiatown born classmate. Both he and I were going to be eighteen in December of that year. September was of quiet demeanour, almost too gentle for the lawless breed that ruled Sophiatown. We had been friends since early childhood. Now we both attended the Krause Street High School in Vrededorp, which lay about two miles from the Johannesburg city centre. Fietas, as Vrededorp was popularly known, was a small, over-populated cosmopolitan ghetto chiefly inhabited by an Indian merchant class and coloured artisans. The mostly Afrikaner whites who lived in the northern section of Vrededorp were poor and badly educated. They occupied cheap, run-down single and semi-detached houses and because of their poverty, the Boers had developed a love-hate relationship with the more affluent Indians. Love for the goods they received on credit, and hate to have Indians as neighbours. Need sometimes makes strange bedfellows. . . .

The Africans — natives as they were called in those days — lived by some inexplicable strategy in the southern corner of Fietas, sand-wiched between their Indian and coloured neighbours, an anomalous group between cosmopolitan Fietas and the whites-only suburb of Mayfair. Not only had the Africans been 'racially' squeezed, but they — and some coloured families — were victims of excessively high and exploitative rentals.

The friends I had made in Fietas had been won or overwhelmed by the force of my fists. They were easy to come by, and this was the reason why September had wanted me to run with him — word was out that the Times Square gang member I had whipped a week before was out to get us. Word was always out but it hardly bothered me. I mused as I passed Mukkadam's butchery. His son Ghalab, had tasted the wrath of my fists inside the classroom after he had called me Hopalong Kaffir — instead of Cassidy because of the way I used to walk. Durango Kid — the boxer I had thrashed — was Ghalab's hero.

The rain began to fall harder and I was compelled to run for a Sophiatown-bound bus.

I sat near a woman who I knew was a new arrival in our street. It was said that she came from the farms in Zululand. Light-skinned and petite, she had short curly hair and a small neat nose with soft dimpled cheeks. Thick eyebrows seemed to protect her big eyes. I had often tried to speak to her because of the powerful sexual urge I experienced whenever she smiled at me. She was delicate and demure, and it made me feel good just looking at her.

'Dumazile,' she responded when I asked her her name. 'Can you speak Zulu?'

'Yes,' I told her, 'but only a little; just enough to tell you that you live in our street.' My Zulu was slow and cautious.

She smiled and silence followed as the bus jerked, braked and skidded to the left and right, so that one minute I would breathe on her and the next she on me. It felt good touching her and feeling her warm, intimate breath on my face. Dumazile, I discovered, had a daughter whose father had been brutally killed during a faction feud in Msinga, Zululand. The man had been much older than her. She had feared for her life and had come to Johannesburg to seek work.

I was totally oblivious to the noise in the bus until a half-drunk man, who had just got on, shouted: 'Baby come *duze*! Come *duze* baby!' He wriggled his hips, pointing at Dumazile then at me. '*Sukuma wena mfana*!' He meant that I should give him my seat. Baby come *duze* was what the sex-starved migrant labourers exhorted whenever they saw a woman they desired. The intruder repeated his command to me to get up from the seat, but as he advanced I pushed him angrily and pulled out my hunter's knife.

'You are playing, *baba* (father); I stand up for nobody! I've paid money just like you.' My Zulu came out fast and angry.

I moved towards the man but Dumazile pulled at me. 'Sit,' she said firmly, 'can't you see he's drunk?'

Then someone shouted at the intruder, 'Be careful, that one is a *tsotsi*; he will *gwaza* (stab) you. This is not Jeppe hostel!' Some people laughed mockingly and I found strength and greater courage in their mockery — they appeared to be on my side.

Dumazile's honour and my manhood would be protected, or so I believed. I sat and looked at her, and her eyes seemed to be reaching into mine.

'I know you are called Don and you live in those big, big houses.' I nodded. 'How old are you?' she asked.

I hesitated, and purposely dropped the knife as if to convince her of my manhood: if I can carry a knife doesn't that make me a man? But I remained silent. She repeated her question.

'Eighteen,' I replied in the hope that it would end the interrogation. But no. . . .

'What standard are you in?' Her English was good.

'Standard eight, J.C.' I lied, as I had about my age. Why the hell must she know, especially as she looked so tiny against me? She smil-

ed her warm and enchanting smile, and told me that she had gone up
to standard ten but had not completed it. When I raised my head, I
looked straight into the intruder's stare. I stared back and sniggered.
He cowered and looked away. Another round won. . . .

Dumazile and I alighted in Toby Street, two streets from our
destination. She lived diagonally opposite our house at number 19.
We walked at her pace. My face was dripping from the rain and my
white school shirt clung to my body. She opened her umbrella and
gave it to me to carry. We walked in silence into our street, then into
Govender's fruit shop for milk and bread. Up we strolled, still at her
pace. People huddled and hurried past us as if they were afraid of
some impending storm. It seemed an eternity before we finally reached my home. It was 6.20 pm, and I knew that nobody would ask
where I'd been, coming back so late from school.

Nobody cared. . . .

I turned to enter our yard and gave back her umbrella. We stopped.

'Are you going home?' she asked, and before I could answer, she
said, 'Come with me; baby come *duze*. . . .' We both laughed. I
shook my head half-reluctantly. 'Come,' she said in Zulu. 'You must
first dry out and have some tea.'

Gerty Street had suddenly become a morgue or a cemetery in the
strange silence. I felt a warm strength between my thighs, rushing hot
into my muscle, so that it pressed hard against my pants. It was a
sensation far deeper than anything I had experienced with the other,
younger girls I used to chase in the dark.

'Come. . . .'

Once at the door to her room, Dumazile unlocked several
padlocks and pulled the huge bolts. We entered the dark, humid
twelve foot square room. My hand felt her bed; she fumbled and rattled a box of matches. The paraffin lamp gave a yellow light to the
room, and to her eyes. She smiled. I took a seat opposite her. The
primus stove obeyed humbly, almost slavishly when she pumped it
and lighted its head so that a blue-and-yellow flame shot upward.
The water boiled; the tea warmed me inside.

'Are you warm now?' she asked.

I nodded and noticed at the same time that the heat between my
legs and the hardness in my muscle were not as intense as they had
been in the street. Strange how it was: heat of the tea cooling the heat

deep down that had made me feel like a real man.

When Dumazile took my shirt, she also took me. She probed again in her mother tongue, 'Have you ever been with a woman before; I mean have you ever slept with a girl?'

Silence.

. . . . Silence is that fleeting period when the soul makes its entry into the embryo, and life comes to the blood; it is also that moment when the soul casts off its human weight and heads towards the Eternal Source. Silence is that pause between Truth and Lie when the heart must choose. . . .

'Don, have you slept with a girl before?'

After what appeared to be a hundred years, I nodded yes, but I was lying — I had never had sex. Masturbated yes, but never slept with a girl, let alone a woman. 'Yes,' I said to reaffirm the lie, and so to endorse my manhood.

'Come. . . .'

That night came with a deep and heavy fire; dark and flaming against my skin and inside my body. I remembered the secret code: 'Baby come *duze*', woman come closer; child, boy, man, draw nearer, come *duze*. Thunder roared from my body and burning lightning flashed through my muscles. Dumazile called my name what seemed to be one thousand times.

'Come. . . .'

The magic word that summoned the fiery night into the twelve-by-twelve room, and severed the golden thread of my virginity. The rain fell much harder. I slept on her breasts; emptied, hurt, ashamed and delightfully bewildered, yet at the same time enveloped in a profound fulfilment of peace, of strength and of a power unrealised. Funny. . . .

'Dumazile,' I asked, 'what is the Zulu word for comfort? What word is there for comfort in your language?'

Silence.

'Is that how you feel, my Don?'

'Yes. . . .' But why always a question with a question, I wondered.

'Well that's how I also feel; comforted.'

Her words had the same mysterious magic I had seen in her eyes.

'But what does it mean in Zulu?'

'Duduza; it means duduza or duduzile.'

'Why it's almost like your name!'

'No, my name Dumazile means disappointment or to be disappointed.'

'Why did your parents call you by that name? Were they disappointed about something? It was my turn to interrogate.

'Yes, my birth. You see my father wanted his first-born child to be a son.'

Silence.

'Well I'm not disappointed,' I said. She gave a soft, almost whispering laugh.

'Yes,' she said and touched my navel. Life and fire surged back once more; dark and flaming from the night. I remember calling her name a thousand, a million times. A new and deep sleep overwhelmed me.

Baby come *duze*. . . .

Several Thursdays followed: woodwork classes and the 'comfort in disappointment' I experienced with Dumazile, caused quite a stir at number 19 and made many people look at me askance. Grown men and women, boys and girls my age, looked and peered and chattered like monkeys. I ignored the talk and went out of my way — gambling and stealing — to give or buy Dumazile those things a lover could give.

It was always difficult to get her to talk about herself because she was so secretive about those things she loved and wanted; things that had given her joy as a child and pain as a woman. I guess that at eighteen there were things I was not supposed to know or feel or even hope to understand. Lots of people, including members of my family, used to say that I was precocious: *ougat* (old arse) as they coarsely put it, because of my intellect and my knowledge of matters which they claimed were adult. Dumazile often told me that she was never quite sure whether to treat me as a young boy or as an adult when it came to discussing serious issues.

The one time she spoke about herself was on Guy Fawkes night, November 5, 1953.

'I come from a strict family — strict and traditional — where we women are often treated as slaves; as pots and pans and calabashes from which to drink water or beer. It is only when a woman becomes much older, *li-Mama* or *li-Gogo* (old mother or granny), that she is held in some esteem. Why wait until I'm old before my dignity as a woman, as a person (*uMuntu*), can be respected? She spoke deeply and almost in pain.

I did not fully comprehend her lamentation on the trials of Zulu womanhood. The look in my eyes may have deceived her into believing that I understood her rebelliousness and her hidden anguish.

She continued: 'Don, how do coloureds treat their women? Do your father and his brothers follow the black tradition of superiority when it comes to coloured women?'

I shook my head. 'I can't really say, Dumazile because in our family, my father and uncles all have black wives. In fact my own mother is black, a Tswana, and I know that there has been ill-treatment of women as well as peace and understanding. My granny was half-Xhosa and my grandfather is an Italian.'

Dumazile nodded, somewhat perplexed. 'Yes,' she said, 'but this is Johannesburg — *Kwa-umfazi ushayi indoda*' (the place where woman beats her man).

'So, you ran away from Natal because women are badly treated there?' I probed, not certain that it was the correct thing to say, and also not wanting to hurt her feelings.

'Partly that, but more because my parents had allowed a man to get off lightly after he raped me on my way home from the mission school. I was about to complete standard ten.'

Dumazile's face assumed a pensiveness I had never seen in her before. I felt deep compassion for her.

'I was also in a mission school in Durban at a place called Mayville. One of the big boys, a chap called Dry, molested me sexually. But I hit him with an iron pipe over the head. Dry bled like a pig and was later expelled from the school.'

My words failed to soothe her; instead her eyes searched my face intently and she recoiled from me.

'I had really wanted to become a nurse,' she said coldly.

. . . To recall hurt or humiliation is not easy. Always there is the risk that the harsh hand of time will rupture the unhealed wounds and lay bare the blood and flesh and the trauma of bitter experiences, when cruel deeds bruised our limbs, and uncaring words tried to kill our human dignity. There is always the risk. . . .

I feared it was for this reason that Dumazile had recoiled from me, had moved back into the safety of her shell, that if she had revealed more, part of her would surely have died. There was always the risk.

But I probed again: 'Was that man ever punished? What did your father do? Did he make the man pay for his crime against you?' My questions rushed out like waves of anger and concern, to show her that I was on her side, on the side of the aggrieved; and — unconsciously — on my own side.

Dumazile nodded and moved closer. Her words had a coldness I shall never forget. 'My father knew the man. He belonged to the same clan as our family: a Sithole. They made him pay damages. He was far older than me, old enough to be my father. I was only nineteen and I did so want to become a nurse.'

'Was that why you did not finish standard ten?' I asked.

'Yes. I became pregnant and the nuns found out and forced me to leave school because of the bad influence on the other girls.'

Dumazile began to cry quietly, and whatever I said, out of helpless confusion perhaps, failed to comfort and ease her pain. But why, why had she told me the story?

'Dumazile,' I asked, 'what happened to that man and the child?'

'The man, thank God, was killed by Zwane clansmen who attacked our village. My father was also brutally killed.'

'Is your child still alive?' I was persistent, and Dumazile drew back once more and asked me to leave the room. It was long past midnight and all the Guy Fawkes revelry in the streets had died down. I went home and stood knocking at the door of my father's room.

'Go back where you came from,' was my father's response. I heard my stepmother giggle. I slept on the verandah of my grandfather's house, angry and bitter and not knowing what would happen between Dumazile and me.

There was always the risk.

One Thursday in mid-November as we walked from the bus stop, Dumazile held my hand tightly. We stopped.

'Don how old are you really?'

'Eighteen. December 29 I'll be nineteen. Why do you ask?'

'Well, I want you to know that I have a daughter almost your age. She's fifteen; in fact she will be sixteen in December on Dingaan's Day.' Dumazile counted sixteen on her fingers and smiled at me devillishly. I remember feeling hurt and embarrassed. A schoolboy pain — something given, something taken back. But I let it ride.

'What is her name?' I asked.

'Duduzile.'

'Comfort?'

'Yes, and she will be at my room when we get there. She has come for money; besides I have missed her.' This time Dumazile spoke Zulu. 'I don't want her to know about us. What would she say if she heard all the gossip about us? You a schoolboy — almost her age; what would she think of me? Don, this business between us has got to stop now!'

I did not know how to respond although I knew she was in earnest. Not see her again! God, I would surely die. But I kept my thoughts to myself.

Duduzile looked a lot like her mother, only taller and stronger, but with identical dimples. Her hair was plaited into thick, shining strips that moved in a circle to end on the crown of her well shaped head. I greeted her in Zulu but she responded in English. I left them, not knowing what would happen the next day. Dumazile's door was locked for the whole of that weekend including the Friday. That weekend was also the first one in a long, long time that saw me take my knife to the streets, and return home at night with my clothes soaked in blood.

My gang members welcomed me. 'Many happy returns. . . .'

Monday died; Tuesday was born; was buried. Wednesday was cremated with the ashes of my burnt out heart. Thursday rose heavy with expectation, a pregnant day, which carried my hope and my fears. I scanned every tired face in the 5.45 pm bus. Then at her home I shook the massive padlocks. Friday died along with all its countless victims of violence and crime perpetrated by *tsotsis*, young thugs like me who used to hide in school uniforms and behind the cassocks of altar boys. Late Saturday afternoon of that tortured week, I bought groceries and meat for Dumazile. The locks were off. I heard voices and without knocking, I pushed the door open and saw a man dressed only in his underpants on the same bed that had brought life and fire to my body; the same bed that was stained with my very substance.

'What the fucking hell!' The man's voice was deep and hoarse.

Dumazile who stood in her favourite blue petticoat quickly banged the door in my face, but I kicked it open and flung the groceries and meat into the room. I ran away, held my hand to my mouth and dashed into a toilet where I vomited my anger, my hurt and humiliation into the pan. I hid in our coalshed and cried bitterly, not understanding my sadness.

I took my knife from its hiding place and vowed that I would get them both. Night brought the fire of anger. I returned to Dumazile's room and waited for them to come outside. I vowed to speak the only language I knew and understood — violence.

'Baby come *duze*; come *duze* baby,' I whispered into the door. Silence. When morning came I peeped into the room. There was no-one inside. For days and weeks, past Dingaan's Day, past Christmas and my birthday, the locks remained on her door.

I never saw her again.

6. Other Faces of Kofifi

A hideous face belonged to squalor or poverty or sickness or death. There was no real difference: the greater part of Sophiatown was a deplorable, sickening slum. Blacks had freehold rights and some houses were comparable to those of whites living in the adjoining suburbs, but Sophiatown was rotting at the core because the Johannesburg City Council did not accept full responsibility for its maintenance. Public amenities such as sports fields, recreational facilities? There wasn't a single football field in the whole township.

Basketball and football were played in the school grounds and in the streets. Church halls, classrooms and zinc shacks became the boxing stables that produced many champions, and killers too. One such boxer was King Berry, who was hanged for brutally murdering his wife because of jealousy. The women composed a song which ran: 'King Berry the champ killed the only thing he loved. He must have been bewitched. . . .'

But Sophiatown also had its beauty; picturesque and intimate like most ghettos. Double-storey mansions and quaint cottages, with attractive, well-tended gardens, stood side by side with rusty wood-and-iron shacks, locked in a fraternal embrace of filth and felony. Among the wealthy were African, coloured, Indian and Chinese people.

One rich man, Mabuza, owned a double-storey house which he filled with the most expensive furniture, to the tune of about thirty thousand pounds. Added to this was a three-storey building with a huge dairy and butchery on the ground floor, five bedrooms on the upper storey and a big restaurant sandwiched between. Mabuza, whose son Early became a famous jazz musician, owned another large restaurant on the outskirts of Johannesburg. In Sophiatown, no-one could choose their neighbours, so that alongside the wealthy Mabuzas or the Xumas or the Makhenes or the Rathebes lived the miserably poor and the wretched. All that the rich could do, at the time, was build high walls with broken glass cemented on top of them to keep out thieves.

The rich and the poor, the exploiters and the exploited, all knitted together in a colourful fabric that ignored race or class structures. The children mixed freely whether their families disagreed or not. Children in their innocence hardly recognised the differences. There were no separate bourgeois areas or élite concert halls, just long streets and thousands of people who moved over each other like restless, voracious insects: blacks exploiting blacks. And what needs the white authorities failed to provide in the way of social amenities, the Catholic and Anglican Churches met at great cost. The rich landlords, among them many whites and Indians, never channelled any part of their huge profits back into the township; it was a dog-eat-dog world, harsh and yet tender in a strange, paradoxical way.

Sophiatown had two Jewish-owned cinemas: the Picture Palace, also named Balanski after its owner, and the Odin owned by a man called Lakier. The Odin was said to be the largest cinema in the whole of Africa, with a seating capacity of about 1 100. It was also used as a concert hall, a church and a venue for mass political meetings by organisations such as the African National Congress, the Anti-Removals Committee, the Defiance of Unjust Laws Campaign Committee. The internationally known singer Miriam Makeba, now in exile and prohibited from returning to South Africa, also performed at the Odin — where knives and guns were carried and often brazenly used by members of the audience. Sometime between 1948 and 1950, while I was at school in Durban, Lakier also opened a Harlem-USA type milk bar and juke-box saloon complete with slot-machines and peer-in movie boxes.

Almost everything we wore or ate was fashioned after American styles. Some gangs and gang members chose the names, habits and mannerisms of film stars such as George Raft, John Garfield and John Wayne, who was nicknamed *Motsamai* (swaggerer). Some fashion shops actually overpriced their clothes on the recommendation of the Americans gang who wanted — and were prepared to pay for — the exclusive privilege of wearing USA imports such as Florsheim, Nunn Bush and Jarman shoes. What they probably did not realise at the time was that the shops would bequeath the high-price legacy into the sixties, seventies and eighties. 'Made in the USA' became the sole criterion and any rubbish that carried the USA label was desirable for that alone. And Sophiatown had many shops and tailors — invariably Jewish or Indian owned — that raked in huge profits on the 'Made in the USA' craze. Even the traditional African herbalists used brightly painted signs to advertise their USA aphrodisiacs, blood mixtures and lucky charms. And if you rejected the American fad, you would quickly be dubbed *moegoe* or greenhorn.

The Face of Religion beamed like colourful fluorescent advertisements from the countless Christian sects and Hindu, Moslem and Buddhist segments that preached and sold their understanding of penitence, redemption and reconciliation with God. There were the rituals of the African *amaZioni* with their frenzied worshipping through cymbals and drums that rose and fell from midnight hour until dawn. Men, women, old and young and children called frantically upon their God as if He was on a long, long holiday. Churches competed for the redemption of souls; trying as it were to sell God at a bargain price to people who had stopped buying, not because they had no money, but because they had no faith. . . .

And salvation was going for a song but men, it appeared were not buying. Only older people opened their ears to listen to the song as they gave the remnants of their wasted and broken lives in final compensatory service to the Great One — the *Umkhulumkhulu*; the *Modimo*, the *Thixo*, who ruled the earth and the sky.

Then there was the mad rattling of tambourines and cymbals, which told of the pace and effort with which people sought refuge from themselves and from beliefs and superstition that were stronger than reason and even Christianity; the throwing of bones or charms often determined a life or a death. Many grew weary of placing the fate of their loved ones, and of their own souls, in the hands of the Unseen God in whose name they were being ruled and reviled. They turned to their traditional doctors when all else failed.

And at dead of night, in the secret of his heart a man will call on his 'doctor'.

Patient: *'Baba, Makhosi* — Father, King there is this thing which troubles my sleep and brings a shadow upon my house. *O Baba, O Makhosi Sizwe* — O Father, O Ruler of our nation I seek your intercession with our sacred *amadhlozi* — our ancestors.'

Doctor: 'I hear you, son of the troubled shadows whose house is without the peace of sleep. These *amathambo* (bones) are the voices of your dead kin; they will reveal to us the thorn of your affliction. In a moment all will be known — nothing is hidden from the *amadhlozi*. Say yes, *vumani-bo*.'

Patient: *'Siya vuma, Makhosi* — We agree, Lord.'

And in the dim, flickering candlelight the *nyanga* (traditional doctor) will mumble his incoherent prayer and solicitation, rattling the sacred bones in his ochrous and beaded hands. The candlelight will move to the heat of his breath; now there, now here. And he will call and pray and invoke the ancient wisdom of his tribe as well as that of his patient's ancestors.

Doctor: *'Makhosi, Makhosi, vumani-bo, vumani-bo!'*

Patient: *'Siya vuma, siya vuma, Makhosi. . . .'*

The bones will then roll onto the sacred rug and the wise tongue lick the eager round lips; the eyes will deepen and stare without a wink. Then will the head shake and the eyes — the perceptive and penetrating eyes — search and scrutinise the position of the bones. Then again and yet again will the bones rattle and dive onto the sacred rug where no foot or shoe may touch.

Doctor: 'Speak *Makhosi,* speak; your son of the shadow troubled by sleeplessness awaits your voice. *Vumani-bo!'*

Patient: '*Siya vuma* (yes). We are united with your spirit!'

Then the bones will speak and the message will be delivered from the face that drips water and the tongue that licks the lips. The patient will listen attentively, and with his head bowed in deference to the presence of something greater than himself, greater than all that lives upon the earth, he will accept the message and await the prescription. The ancestors have spoken through their messenger. *Siya vuma*, we are obedient. . . .

Perhaps the ancestors will demand a life for the 'life' that is given to the patient; blood for blood. Then only will the shadows go to sleep and peace be restored.

And the man or the child or the woman or the lamb or the goat will be slaughtered and the blood be given up. Then shall the shadows walk no more, and then will the long sleep return to purge the pain and the fear.

Vumani-bo, vumani-bo. . . .

The Roman Catholic and the Anglican, the Methodist and Lutheran Churches towered above the splintered Christian groupings like great pillars of strength. Ordered, organised. But badly outnumbered though respected by the various sects as the cradle of their adopted Christian faiths. But was their own African religion not older than the one the early Christian pioneers had brought to Africa from across the great waters? And was it not their own African worship that called the lightning and thunder and the rain when the land was warped and wanting? *Vumani-bo, Makhosi!*

The Catholics and the Anglicans built huge mission schools alongside their churches, as did the Lutherans and the Methodists — all with funds provided by their white sponsors inside South Africa and across the seas. These parent Churches had strong Christian commitments to human dignity and social justice which were epitomised in men and women, nuns and priests, such as Fathers Rakale, Singleton, Sidebotham and Trevor Huddleston whose personal contribution to the people of Sophiatown cannot adequately be expressed on paper.

But as I saw the good among the men of the cloth, so too did I see the bad and the evil. Preachers among the Christian sects used their churches for personal, financial or sexual gain. They accrued vast wealth in the name of God; sold bibles, crosses, ornaments and salvation rods covered with bright cloth, as well as leopard skins and sashes. Some clergymen had many women and actually ordered others to leave their homes and follow the Church — inevitably to bed. The preachers bought cars and lived in huge mansions — their cabins in the sky. All in His name. . . .

And people understood and accepted this as 'the will of God'. This was Sophiatown, where God was going for a song; going at a bargain price. . . . *'Vumani-bo, siya vuma!'*

A swimming pool can be an oasis of fun and revelry to under-privileged children who have no recreation except football, boxing and street-fighting — if the latter can be seen as recreation. The pool then becomes a central meeting place where the bottled energies and frustrations peculiar to children living in a desert of hopelessness can be released.

The pool at the Anglican Church's St Cyprian's Primary School in Meyer Street attracted children from far and wide. All hues, all shapes and sizes flocked faithfully — like war-torn and weather-beaten refugees to 'San Ceepee', as the school was called. 'Dipping pool' would have been more appropriate because overcrowding made swimming virtually impossible. Diving also had its risks. You would be wading on top of somebody and the next minute another dark body would dive on you as if you were invisible. But the pool brought us together — children of the rich and the poor, and the orphans, to expend our energies and renew those links that the Group Areas laws had severed through forced separation. It was also a place for pranks and mischievousness.

A friend of mine, Tolla-Tolla, once brought a small beehive to the pool. Many boys who could not afford swimming trunks were allow-ed to swim naked, and so we waited until the pool was teeming with children. Tolla-Tolla covered his head with a huge towel and flung the bees into the pool. Talk about a quick evacuation! In no time the place was deserted but for a few brave heads that bobbed up out of the water — bees or no bees — for those vital whiffs of fresh air. Priests and pranksters scattered for the safety of the toilets, washrooms and vestries as the angry insects attacked everybody in-cluding the parish cats and canines. What Tolla-Tolla's head did not receive in stings, his exposed bottom got abundantly. My eyes were so badly puffed that I was admitted to hospital. On my return to the pool two weeks after the incident, I was roundly condemned, and

received a few strokes from Father Rakale's thick belt. I was prohibited from using the pool for several weeks. But Tolla-Tolla was
not. At the pool, he smiled wryly at me.

'My head was covered, boy. What they can't see they can't
blame,' he said, tapped me on the head and jumped into the water.

My behaviour improved to the point where I was trained as a life-
saver and sadly helped to retrieve the bodies of a girl and a boy in a
single week.

The Anglicans also operated a small but comprehensive school
library, from which I borrowed my first copy of Peter Abrahams's
Tell Freedom and *Native Son* by the late Richard Wright; books borrowed but shamefully not returned. They made an impression on me
which was to help influence my thinking. From Ekhutuleni soup kitchen, behind the chapel, the nuns distributed food rations which my
Tswana cousins and I collected for the family. We were also given
two slices of bread each, thickly smeared with peanut butter or jam,
and a mug of milk — all with the compliments of Father Huddleston's African Children's Feeding Scheme. The Catholic Church
offered literacy classes for young and old as well as film shows and a
library which was housed inside a nunnery called Notre Dame.

What Sophiatown lacked in recreation halls and sportsfields
Western Native Township had in abundance: an up-to-date library
with lots of reading and study space and neat desks and chairs; a
community hall and a well-equipped youth centre. There were three
football fields, two tennis courts, a cloakroom fitted with toilets and
showers and a huge centrally-situated public washroom with baths
and showers. I recall with a feeling of deep nostalgic joy the legendary Dorcas creche in Western where, as a child of about five years, I
was cared for after being lost for a week. The township also had
spacious lawns and beautiful pine, fir and bluegum trees — all well
tended and trimmed — and a children's park, complete with swings,
see-saws, slides and rocking horses.

There was a massive exodus to Western on certain weekdays and
especially on Sundays, for those traditionally rival football matches
that often ended with brawls when police vehicles, with swinging
doors from which hung laughing, excited constables, would zoom
onto the field and with their whistles screaming law and order, would
chase and grab anything on two feet.

And as the people ran, if you were looking far enough beyond the dust of the speeding police vans and the running feet, you could see the setting sun roll and fall gently into a hole at the southern edge of Western Township to give birth to his neuter offspring called twilight. Then you could see the fading shadows and the silhouettes of tired sportsmen and their supporters trudge wearily through the surreal cloud of dust. People and their dogs moving homeward; children asleep on their mothers' backs moving from light into semi-darkness and finally into night itself; half free, half slaves.

And if you were listening hard enough with your heart and ears close to the breast of the night, you would hear the strong chorus of chirping crickets greeting mankind. Yes, only if you were looking beyond the screeching police vehicles and the dust of running, anxious feet were you part of that wondrous transition.

No foreigner ever visited Sophiatown and remained quite the same, or left South Africa untouched by the unfathomable magic of the condemned township, and the madness that throbbed in its restless brain. In January 1942, while the Allied forces battled tirelessly against the German army — which was openly supported and abetted in South Africa by the fifth column *Ossewa Brandwag* — an unnamed cleric of the Anglican Church in London visited our country. He stayed for several weeks in Sophiatown's Priory of Christ The King in Meyer Street. The priest administered the sacraments to his melanic flock and trudged all over the sprawling township, meeting and talking to people from all walks and pitfalls of life. Before his return to England, he wrote a short piece on Meyer Street, Sophiatown which appeared in *The Star*. 'A Little Glimpse of Sophiatown' may illustrate the bewitching effect that Kofifi had on people.

'. . . I have found a street in this city which is unique in my experience of streets. I have seen nothing like it in London or in all England, or in France, or in Spain, or still less in Australia, which is the other new country I know. Just as the average Londoner has never been to Madame Tussaud's or the Tower, so it occurs to me that most Johannesburg people may never have been to Meyer Street, Sophiatown. If you wish to explore, you can take the Newlands car to stop No. 36, and it is on your right. The beginning of the street is ordinary enough, running uphill for 200 yards, with tarmac and footpaths and gutters. After that there are no footpaths, no gutters, no tarmac and the houses are innocent of water-borne sewage. You had best look where you are stepping, partly because the road is rocky and there are a good many loose stones, and partly because of the local dustbins. If you go, as I did, on a Saturday afternoon, you will find it extremely populous. The street mounts sharply, and if you pick your way to the top you will find a church, a school, a hospital, a house called 'Ekuteleni', where lady workers live, and a clergy house, which may be why my steps were dogged by grubby urchins who grinned at me and said, 'How d'you do, Farder? Goodbye, Farder! Good afternoon, Farder!'

At the top of the hill the street drops, and the intrepid explorer finds an outcrop of rock. If you came thus far by car you made a mistake and you had better get out, because there is no way through for a car. However, you can walk down and cross the intersection of Edward Road. Then, straight ahead of you, there is a pond. I can't help thinking that if you want ponds in your streets they would look better if they were not quite so oozy and slimy. This one is deepest along by the containing wall in front of some houses, and is about three-quarters of the width of the street. At the moment it is about 50 yards long, but I daresay if the weather turns dry there may be rather less water and rather more smell.

It happened I wanted a small job done, so I turned into a yard which had a notice, 'Boot and Shoemaker herein. Beware of the dog. Trespassers will be prosecuted.' There was a smell of hens. A man met me and said, 'No. He's been gone from here a long time.' The smell was asserting itself. I fled, and walked the rest of the way to the end of Meyer Street. It ends abruptly with high iron railings with spikes at the top. If you peep through the railings you see the country, clean and unspoilt.

That, no doubt, symbolises something; but what?. . .'

Other men of the sacred cloth also visited Sophiatown to see first-hand what their parliamentarian representatives called 'the place of sin and iniquity' and 'the cyst of the cancer of communism'. The mission of these Pharisees was not to clothe; to feed; to comfort; to share; to visit and to bury 'the least of God's creations'. No, they came that the scriptures of apartheid might be fulfilled in their granite temples and in their parliament. This was the law; blind to pain and blind to human beauty. They came only that the scriptures of power and separation might be fulfilled according to the Covenant of their austere and unsmiling God.

It was the Law. . . .

7. Father Trevor Huddleston

*O*n Sundays Sophiatown underwent an almost mysterious transformation. The streets seethed with a great mass of people who moved about restlessly and rapidly as if driven by unseen demons and angels who may have been competing for the possession of their souls. Up and down they moved in search of themselves and of God; when only the night before, and until the early hours of magical Sunday, they had swooned and danced the sexual, indigenous *famu* or Marabi dance — a dance of carnal love and passion in which the seductive eyes of woman glowed while she shook her body in its short scanty dress to the delight of the half-drunk man who would take her and pay the price. Marabi and the staring eyes silenced by the ringing of early church bells. Time for cleansing; time for Jesus as men, women and their children marched to church to be made whole of their sinning and debauchery, and then returned for another week of sin and debauchery. This was Sophiatown on a Sunday; a spectacle of clean clothes and big, colourful hats and fancy handbags, and proud fathers who carried their children or held their hands.

I was inside Shorty's Fish and Chips reading the Anti-Removals Committee's pamphlet, when an Indian property owner I knew entered the shop. He saluted thumb raised and the people responded *'Mayibuye!'* He left and crossed the street towards the Odin cinema.

A huge, noisy crowd had gathered and the usual police pick-up vans shot past, blaring their hooters so that people jumped onto the pavement. A large bird flew into the shop and frightened the customers. Women screamed and dashed outside. A burly man who owned a carpentry shop at the corner of Victoria and Gerty Streets trapped the bird and wrung its neck so that its hot blood dripped through his thick fingers. He threw it into the gutter and trampled it viciously until it was a pulp of blood and feathers. Someone shouted: 'That bird had no business here, it was sent by the enemy!' A woman nodded: 'Must be; for what does a bird know about fish and chips?' There was a loud, slow murmur. People nodded in approval.

This was Kofifi; cruel and superstitious. Sunday brought out the best and the worst in people. . . .

Robert Resha of the African National Congress had asked a group of us to hand out the anti-removals pamphlets and had promised to pay. Up Good Street, where the cinema was situated, into Victoria Street and along Annadale Street we walked and handed out the papers until we reached Edward Road which ran parallel to Victoria Street. Then back to the cinema. People would not refuse pamphlets given to them by street thugs like myself; it would be risky. At the cinema we distributed more. The people were entering like thick black syrup with specks of whites, Indians and coloureds in an almost carnival atmosphere. Cameras clicked incessantly. It was the big day in February of 1955, and my fifth year of street-fights and public violence and intermittent arrest. The crowd parted suddenly as if to form a guard of honour. Some men took off their hats, and young and older women moved back silently, almost in reverence. Here was the man, loved respected and revered. A giant who strode high, hard and heavy through the pews and corridors of influential places, and yet touched the earth with the humility he was endowed with through his faith and calling as a servant of God.

Father Trevor Huddleston, who was born in Bedford, England in 1913. Before he came to South Africa in 1943 to head the Church of England's Community of the Resurrection in Sophiatown, he was a missionary in Ceylon and India. Father Huddleston, whom children in Sophiatown used to call FAADAA, was ordained as a priest in 1937. I was familiar with the Anglican Church of St Cyprian's where my Tswana family had worshipped, and where as a child I had accompanied them to collect parcels of food rations. A priest called Singleton had sent my cousin Dutch and me to the Margaret Ballinger Home in Roodepoort beyond Sophiatown, west of Johannesburg.

And as the people gave way for him to pass, I remember moving towards him and I stood almost in his path. His long, bony fingers rubbed my hair and he smiled deeply and seriously. He had made a reputation for himself as an outspoken foe of the policy of apartheid, as well as of crime and violence especially among black people. He had helped build the swimming pool at the Anglican Church's premises in Sophiatown; he had helped found a jazz band that was named after him. And so the 'dauntless one' passed me and entered the main hall, with a smile that was deep and serious.

Hard, brittle men ushered the people to their seats. The banners of the ANC, the Anti-Removals Committee and the Transvaal Indian Congress hung from the curtain and on each side of the stage. Several men and a woman, who appeared to be high-ranking officials, sat on chairs behind a long table. Two white men sat on chairs near some steps, with Father Huddleston to their right. Several jugs of water and glasses were neatly set out. There would be a lot of talking.

Dan Siwisa the tailor, a short man who was a friend of our family, and of the late John B. Marks, stood and briefly addressed the crowd. Then a tall, wiry man stood up and shouted, *'Mayibuye iAfrika!'* Thunderous, deafening response shook the hall, so that my skin crawled.

'My people,' began Siwisa, 'brothers and sisters of Africa, we are here to reaffirm our allegiance to our land and our countrymen. Let us in song ask God's blessing so that our land and our children, and their children's children, can someday know total freedom.' The response was almost a war-cry, resonant and awesome. Then came the singing of the sacred anthem, Nkosi Sikelele iAfrika (God Bless Africa). First the delicate shrill of the women's voices that appeared to be rolling from the slopes and grassy hillocks of our land, to burst into thin, melodic sound, then to be raised to the ceiling of the hall by the sonorous baritones of the men. The lifting was gentle though; as a giant would lift a child — gently yet firmly. And those who did not understand the words moved with the fulfilling rhythm.

. . . I tell you, there is something in the human voice that can puzzle the mind. Something which diminishes weight and measure, lifting you to heights unknown, undreamed of; where you search for God in others and feel Him in yourself. . . .

I saw a woman dressed in the full ANC uniform weep steady tears as she sang. I understood the song, but not why she cried. Most of the women in her row were crying as well. Perhaps the anthem had affected them strangely, for the tears came like *medupe* — gentle rain — without the booming crack of thunder. Crying yes, but not the kind that comes with hurt; the soft, happy tears that follow childbirth. A joy born out of pain. Women are strange.

'Save Africa. Why Africa, when it is the people dying and losing their homes, their possessions and their birthright?' The lanky man's voice reverberated through the hall so that many heads nodded their agreement. He continued: 'The government imposes its will upon the people through violence and bloodshed. I say an eye for an eye; I say a life for a life *Mayibuye!*' He vanished into the crowd amid roaring applause and shouts of *'Mayibuye iAfrika!'* More than a thousand thumbs shot up into the air; one of them belonged to the wife of a black special branch policeman called Jerry Mollson who lived in Sophiatown. Other speakers rose; their themes hardly varied:

> Injustice
> Slavery
> Exploitation
> Expropriation of properties
> Domination

Freedom and human dignity, and the recognition of black people's rights to own homes and live without the threat of being forcibly removed from their properties and houses by the police and the government's military forces.

Some people spoke of bloodshed and the need for arms if the might of the African, coloured and Indian masses were to mean something. One Indian speaker who was introduced to the audience as the leader of the Transvaal Indian Congress, and a member of the Defiance of Unjust Laws Campaign, spoke vehemently about the threat of expropriation and misappropriation of properties. He said Dr Xuma and Oliver Tambo, in the company of Duma Nokwe, would outline a plan by the Anti-Removals Committee to fight the land/property issue in the highest courts of the country. He bitterly attacked the Prime Minister, Hans Strijdom and his lieutenant at the time, Hendrik Verwoerd. Police special branch officer Spengler also came in for a vitriolic tongue-lashing which raised the crowd to their feet amid great applause and shouting.

I heard things I had not imagined possible; men shouting vehemently and with such open anger, men I had seen tipping their hats to white policemen and government officials: 'I'm not one of them, my *baas.* . . .' This was something new. I was beginning to discover what strange things politics do to men.

There was a hush when Father Huddleston stood to speak. Like many others, I had only heard him give sermons, and had read about him in newspapers. When he spoke a thrill of expectation lashed at my temples. My throat burned with a dryness that was not really a dryness, but something hard to swallow. He told the audience that much of what the speakers before him had said was true. 'The National Party government has failed in many respects to meet the legitimate demands of the oppressed people. I am as angry as you are when your homes are being destroyed in the name of Christianity while we know it is really in the name of apartheid.' He said that although the evils were perpetrated by white people, not all whites were evil. There were some who were mindful of the suffering and tribulations of the black people. He said he opposed the removals because of the ideological motives of the authorities which they paraded as humanitarian.

'Daily you are being tested and tempted into violence by the authorities, but that would be a great folly because violence only begets violence.' He urged the people to stand together and unite.

While he spoke uniformed and plain-clothes policmen, all armed, entered the hall and approached the outspoken Indian leader who had attacked Verwoerd and Strijdom. They ordered him to accompany them but he refused and exchanged words with them. And in full view of the crowd, a tall, pipe-smoking, detective in a hat grabbed the Indian leader by the arm, pulled him from the stage and walked towards the exit. His quarry stumbled and fell. A woman near him screamed. The crowd rose as one person and shouted abuse at the police captors; some rushed out of their seats and fell over each other in their advance towards the police, who hurriedly lifted their captive. I instinctively removed my knife from its pouch and headed for the exit: if there was to be violence, then I would be part of it because I understand it better than the politics which had made the women cry, and so greatly angered their menfolk.

I heard people shout: *'Skiet! Skiet!'* (Shoot! Shoot!) Once outside the hall I saw men and women advance angrily towards the policemen who in turn brandished handguns and submachine guns. *'Staan weg!'* (Stand aside!) they warned the crowd. But obscenities drowned their voices. And behind them several bystanders joined in the shouting. Any moment now, I thought, and glimpses of the tram fare riots flashed through my mind — when people had fought the police and government authorities over a penny increase. Always it had been the police and the people; always the armed and the unarmed — guns against stones. I waited with perverted expectation and desire for the captors to shoot at us. I wanted to see the familiar hand shoot the familiar shot; wanted to see the familiar limp body drenched in its own blood. I moved up to the front row, my knife held firmly.

Any time now. . . .

Father Huddleston pushed madly through the crowd, his big wooden rosary firm in the thick belt around his waist.

'Wait,' he shouted, 'we must not have violence here!' Both factions froze, momentarily suspended. Grim expressions fell like heavy rags. The priest crossed the invisible line of trenches between the two warring forces and spoke to the tall pipe smoker who held a revolver in one hand and his quarry in the other. Another policeman showed the priest a piece of paper and folded it. Father Huddleston then turned to the crowd and pleaded with them to return to the hall, where the meeting would be continued. The police lowered their weapons and part of the crowd moved cautiously until they were inside. A man bit his lip; a frown showed on his face, disturbing yet akin to the expectation and desire I had felt when the police first brandished their guns. I remained outside and watched them drive away, their bespectacled quarry huddled in the back seat between two burly, sour-faced detectives. Then the anthem rang out again; more plaintive, more profound, surging into the blood with the warmth that Nkosi Sikelele always evokes.

When the people came out, they began singing their sarcastic political rally ditties, scorning and poking fun at the authorities. Smartly dressed in their khaki and gaberdine uniforms, black berets and green, gold and black tabs on their shoulders, the women marched and sang from their hearts. Some young men proudly carried poles from which fluttered huge flags of the national movement.

I watched the lanky priest with the bony fingers and aquiline features move through the crowd. He appeared to be tired and I felt a strange love and pity for the man. What force was there in him, that made others succumb?

Even the police whom I had challenged and fought in the streets had heeded and feared him. In my gang, the Vultures, one word from me, one careless instruction to any gang member, determined whether an enemy lived or died. Admiration pounded in my heart and I followed him from a distance, my knife tucked secretly under my shirt. And from nowhere the greetings began, until a huge crowd of children were following the priest as if he were a religious Pied Piper. Some of them touched his heavy black robe and the rosary that swung from his belt. More courageous ones shook his pale hands. Others made the sign of the cross, and took me back to the confessional of the Catholic Church where I repeated my creed of contrition like a parrot: 'Bless me, Father for I have sinned against God. . . .'

I watched the priest smile; his deep, grave eyes changed before the innocence of childish abandon and joy. In that moment I made myself believe that he was happy; or that happiness could flow out of a man who had earlier that day averted bloodshed.

. . .I tell you, strange distant drums beat in the heart when love and admiration surge forth, giving rise to emotions deeper than you can understand. And because you are both men, both warriors in different armour, you hold your peace; loving and admiring in silence. . . .

February 1955 was the time when the first seeds of real political awareness were planted in me and in a few of my friends. It was also my most violent year. I was nearly twenty and without any real hope in sight for my rehabilitation — at least that was what many people said and feared. In April of that year I was shot twice. On the night of the fourth, a police bullet badly grazed my calf during an attack on a police vehicle. The next morning, an Indian schoolteacher shot me through the thigh after his first bullet had missed its mark and hit a school satchel I was holding. On November 5, I led an attack on a municipal police office to rescue a member of our gang. Several people were hurt. Then on November 11 I shot at a township guard and during my escape I was overpowered and stabbed several times by a rival gang member. Nineteen days later he was dead. On December 19 of the same year, I was arrested and charged with his murder. I spent that Christmas as well as my twentieth birthday in prison in the company of convicted criminals among whom were rapists and vicious killers.

I was the first of eleven accused. Yet ironically, those words spoken at that anti-removals meeting were not to be in vain. Years later I was to attend political and education lectures and repeat the fiery speeches of that meeting at rallies and youth gatherings throughout the Transvaal. I would also read my poems of protest and resistance in university halls and from township platforms. But that is another story. . . .

Father Huddleston was an integral and important figure in the life and history of Sophiatown and the country as a whole. His active and selfless role stands as a monument of human concern over the sordid plight of the Newclare squatters, which he has graphically described in his moving, uncompromising book *Naught for Your Comfort*. He was as 'Kofifi' as the rest of the *outies* (city slickers) of that legendary township. He was a symbol of hope for a land gripped by racial animosity and fear; a friend of the lost and lonely, the rejected and the despised, the least of God's creations.

The Afrikaners called a negrophile a *kafferboetie* (brother of kaffirs) and once during the 1955 removals in Bertha Street on a rainy day, I saw him lift young children onto an army truck. He was quiet and pensive that day and the Boer official, Potgieter, sniggered and laughed at the priest whose black coat was glistening with raindrops and, I would like to think, with tears.

Father Huddleston was severely hounded and harassed by the South African authorities. Death-threats, being stopped in the streets, having his many black and white supporters threatened during his campaign for the African Children's Feeding Scheme are but a few of the known acts of persecution he suffered. Two months after my acquittal and release on the murder charge, in April of 1956, Father Huddleston left South Africa. He had been recalled to his country to take up another post. Some people claimed that he was on the Afrikaner Broederbond hit-list at the time, and that his friends in England had feared for his life. His commitment to his faith was unlike the Christian lip-service preached from the hypocritical pulpits of his and of our day. Let him speak for himself in *Naught for Your Comfort* of the struggle for the freedom and dignity of his flock in South Africa:

> Always, all through the twelve years I have spent in Africa, there has been something constructive to do with and for the people I have loved. The African Children's Feeding Scheme; The Orlando Swimming Bath; The Newclare Squatters; The Huddleston Jazz Band . . . Absorbing and fascinating and exciting, all of them. But I do not think they would have been enough to lift the weight of sorrow from my heart, had it not been for the daily and hourly knowledge of African friendship and affection. Often enough, I confess it with deep shame, I have been impatient, angry even, at the incessant interruptions and claims upon 'my' time. But God knows I would not have been without a moment of it. I have never understood or been able to understand how White South Africa can so lightly forfeit such a richness of life; can, on the contrary, build around itself such mighty and impenetrable barriers of pride and prejudice and fear. At least I do understand.'

Perhaps my sharpest memory of him was soon after I came back for good from the Catholic convent school in Durban. One Sunday I found my way to a church in Ray Street. There was incense, and little bells rang at intervals during the service, but the communion wine was sipped by all the communicants, not just the priest, and I realised this was not a traditional Catholic Mass.

Afterwards, the priest stood at the door and greeted the congregation as we came out. When everyone had left and I was alone with the priest, I asked: 'Father, is this a Catholic church?'

'No, this is the Anglican Church, my son. The Catholic church is in Annadale Street.'

So Father, which is the right Church, the Anglican or the Catholic, because I come from a Catholic school, and they told us the Catholic Church is the true Church of God?'

Father Huddleston smiled and shook his head very gently. I repeated my question.

He then rubbed my head tenderly, and pressed the long bony forefinger of his right hand into my ribs, where my heart was beating fast.

'There, my son, there, in your heart, is the true Church of God.'

8. Pinocchio

*T*he terror and trauma of South African apartheid brutality was for me, never so poignantly nor so tellingly told as in the tragi-comic story of a Sophiatown jazz lover and record collector called 'Pinocchio'. Small, almost dwarfish, but with an unusually large, shining forehead, he spoke softly, with an amiability that easily won friends. Pinocchio belonged to what we thugs at the time dubbed 'The Nylon Club'. These were the peace-loving highbrows whose main interests were wine, woman and song; jazz in this instance. The Nylons were favourites with the *'ousies'* or the *'Motaras',* as the fast-living, hedonistic women were called in Sophiatown during the mid-fifties. The diminutive, colourful man had a sense of joy about him that was so contagious, one could not stop to speak to him without parting in laughter. Yet there was also a tinge of tragic mirth in his eyes; in the way he moved his head and in the way he used to purse his lips.

No story of Sophiatown would mean anything, could ever be real, without Pinocchio because he was a special person; alive and funny and lost. A dreamer and a comic who touched hearts, and made people laugh. . . . The strong, the cunning and the cruel, tough men who ruled the streets, as well as the feeble hearted, everybody respected Pinocchio. Sometimes when we came from our midnight street battles, we would see the solitary, impish figure walking the quiet and subdued alleys of the township without the fear or bother of danger. Walking and whistling a blues number by that arch woman-hater Louis Jordan:

The streets are filled with women looking for romance
And if you ain't got a dollar
Brother you don't stand a chance. . . .'

The little man would sing out loud; the darkness his stage and the bright, shimmering stars his audience.

When we came closer to him the familiar salutation would ring out at us: 'Howdee cats; ya all out on da usual prowl ta-nite eh? Hope ya all git home in one piece and not in pieces. Git that! Sweet, gents. . . .' And with shoes tapping Fred Astaire, Pinocchio would vanish into another alley; another death-trap, another graveyard.

. . . Sometimes laughter and comedy are but the palliatives we carry around with us; masks to shelter and conceal our pain and contusions, our failures and the shards of broken dreams that lie scattered in our hearts. But in some quiet corner, when noise and sound are buried in the coffin of an ancient tranquility and the mask is removed and the clay washed away: oh how frightened the eyes that are alone. . . .

Pinocchio, whose name was Cameron Mokaleng, always dressed like a French painter complete with long, brightly coloured scarf and black beret. His pint-size pants were held in place by braces as well as a thick leather belt which appeared to be choking his waist. His bright shoes were so pointed that some of his close friends often teased that the police would arrest him for carrying dangerous weapons. his parents were not really known to us and rumour had it that Pinocchio had fallen out of the sky on a night that was black as tar, and that in place of a baby's rattle, he had a musical instrument in his hands. Nobody dared to tell him the story although I guessed that he had heard it somehow. Pinocchio also never uttered a word about his folks either. He often referred to Sophiatown as his 'mother', his 'old lady'.

She it was who nurtured his small frame and gave fire to his dreams of someday leaving the cruel land of separation and bigotry and becoming somebody. But his mother, Kofifi, who was also mother and 'lover' to thousands of other dreamers and non-dreamers — good and bad alike — was being butchered by the white man's fear and greed. The house that Pinocchio rented was, without his knowledge or prior warning, sold or misappropriated by the Afrikaner government. Whatever belongings he had, our little man packed and moved, and carried with him a useless, impotent anger.

Like a lost nomad in a desert of despair, Pinocchio lived from one threatened and demolished street to another; his mother, bowed and finally brought to her knees, had fought a losing battle; a battle where white might was right and black lives expendable.

The year was 1958, and Sophiatown was being murdered quietly but with a viciousness so calculated, the pain showed on the faces of sensitive and perceptive wanderers such as Pinocchio. The little man, who looked French but spoke like an American, became utterly disillusioned and displaced amid the rubble and debris of crumbling buildings; of silenced schools and conquered places of religious worship. The man, the music lover, the comic and the dreamer who had infected Sophiatown with his gregarious warmth and humaneness, became querulous and bitter.

Gone were the laughter and the comedy; gone the palliative and the mask. Pain had stripped all bare. The last house he lived in was a tumbledown shack in Meyer Street, not far from the Anglican Rectory of Christ The King. Destitute, unemployed and penniless, Pinocchio alienated and estranged himself from his Sophiatown friends, and joined a group led by a prolific saxophonist called Kippie Morolong Moeketsi (now dead). Kippie had travelled to London with the legendary musical drama 'King Kong'.

Kippie, who in turn teamed up with Cape Town-born jazz pianist extraordinary Dollar Brand (now Abdullah Ibrahim), promised to take Pinocchio with him to the 'fairest Cape and Mother City' of racist South Africa. Hungry and homeless, the little man prepared himself for what was the only way out: 'Leave Sophia alone and go to a place where we'd stay in peace. . .' or so the words of Miriam Makeba's song wailed at the time. The Cape at least had several ports; and with ships sailing to and from the teeming harbours, who could say what the future held. His planned exodus from the City of Gold was accelerated when his demonic pass (also called reference book), *fell* to pieces. Attempts to have it renewed ended tragically. Pinocchio was 'endorsed' out; expelled from Johannesburg under a law that the white parliament had specifically enacted for people who refused to live in Meadowlands. Repatriation to some God-forsaken piece of dry homeland — 'reserve' in those days — was more than Pinocchio could take.

Like his pass — we used to call it 'zangaan' or 'stinka' in the old Sophiatown jargon — Pinocchio fell to pieces. He used to speak with an aching bitterness about remaining in the township. He had had a bellyful. *Adieu* Kofifi, goodbye to his old lady, his beautiful but cruel mother. And once he arrived in Cape Town, the short man with the tall, tall, dreams; a man without a home, without a family and almost without hope, he boarded a ship bound for England as a stowaway from the land of apartheid.

Adieu, goodbye forever.

The ship reached Southampton carrying a little man's heart heavy with the hope of better days, and a burning pain for the mother he had left behind, had forsaken because he grew tired of wearing the masks of laughter and comedy while people were dying around him.

Adieu, farewell Kofifi. . . .

9. Gangland

'**M**aglera', 'Sidikidiki'. . . nobody to this day can say why Newclare, the sprawling ghetto step-sister of Western Native Township, was called by those names. But one thing the fearful — or indifferent — people knew with great certainty was that Newclare was a hell-hole of violence and crime. It spawned some of the most vicious and cold-blooded knifemen and gangsters Johannesburg's black townships had ever known. So daring and reckless were their exploits that they made Sophiatown's big shots look like kindergarten crooks. The violence of Newclare had its roots in the pre-Second World War period when huge Basotho clans roamed the streets bullying people and demanding protection fees. A group of gambling city slickers who grouped together for common survival declared war on the Basotho thugs whose groups went by strange names such as the Ghost Raiders and the Vanishing Brigade (later called the Vanishing).

One tough guy with special boxing skills — he served time in jail with my father — was known as 'Jigga Jake'. His reputation spread to Sophiatown and Johannesburg proper and in no time he built a huge following and gave a criminal haven to many seasoned thugs as well as up-and-coming *tsotsis*. His dreaded Jakes Gang came into being. They conquered and controlled several other outfits during the War years. Bra Jake was arrested, tried and convicted for two murders which my father used to say were 'done on reason'. Apparently his woman had cheated on him and during an attack into the *'Rooi Jaart'* (Red Yard) — the vice and sex den of the Ghost Raiders, he found her in bed with another man. People say Jake stabbed her more times than Julius Caesar's assassins stabbed him. Her new lover suffered the same gruesome fate. Jake was given a double life sentence in the winter of 1946. One scourge had been removed from the impoverished and beleaguered community. There was peace.

But soon other menaces reared their heads in Newclare. The reputation of Bra Jigga Jake — his callousness and cruelty, his criminal genius and his power over women — was pushed out of memory by the next big name.

Chops Number One was a thug who fearlessly walked the slimy streets of Newclare. He was a man of criminal bravado and often took on two or more rivals in knife battles. Scarred and wounded, he would still put his adversaries to flight. People forgot Jake. Chops Number One was the only name uttered in fear and open admiration. He had a way with young kids — always giving them cash and presents. He used the children as his informers and took some of them into his outfit after their 'graduation' from fist fights to the bloody gang warfare that plagued Newclare.

One day, Chops Number One's woman was assaulted by a rival. Chops butchered him. The man's dying words to his relatives were, 'Chops attacked me. . . tell my mother it was Chops who killed me.' On the strength of those fatal words, Chops Number One *'Die Bushie van K.Y.'* (the Bushman from Kimberley) was tried and sentenced to death.

He was hanged. But violence did not swing with him on the rope. Number One was dead. Number Four came and went. Number Five

made his presence felt in 1954 against my gang. He died of poisoning
in jail. I was spared to tell this story but I carry many marks on my
body — knife and gunshot wounds — reminders of a time when the
only heroes we loved and worshipped, feared or emulated were
killers whose only classroom was the street and whose only code of
conduct and survival was violence.

We knew no other life except brutality and bloodshed. Whether
you used your fists, or weapons, you knew it was the only way to
survive. Freedom and justice meant what the streets wanted them to
mean. We had heard and seen Luthuli in the Freedom Squares of
Newclare and Sophiatown; we had heard Xuma and Nyembezi
speak. John B. Marks had lived in Newclare which Moses Kotane,
Dadoo, Sacks and a lawyer called Fischer had visited frequently to
address the crowds. But to a boy with a knife in his pocket they were
just names in the foul air of the ghetto.

Freedom and justice. . . . What did they mean when a policeman
was shooting at you in the dark? When you ran but kept a count of
the shots fired at you so that you could turn back and challenge the
bastard, and then tell the story to your comrades?

Freedom and justice can only mean something to a boy when that
boy has been taught to mean something to himself. Freedom and
justice are as vital and necessary to a man or a boy as systole and
diastole are to the human body. Why did God spare me among so
many? And why did I find a deeper bitterness and fear, and
loneliness and alienation in politics, that did not exist in the gang
warfare of the slum streets?

To have been a young street fighter or a thug or gangster in the
ghettos of Sophiatown, Alexandra Township or Vrededorp, or any
other black slum throughout the length and breadth of the country
was to be the victim of dehumanisation. We were animals trapped in
cages of human indifference. But for a few individuals — among
them teachers, nuns and churchmen — nobody really cared about
us. In many instances families instead of chastising their delinquent
children actually goaded them on to commit acts of violence, and
'profitable' crimes such as theft, robbery and burglary. A great
number of parents — themselves stripped of common decency either
through human weakness or as a result of the policy of apartheid —
lived unashamedly off the criminality of their misguided — unguided
children, at times even hiding the bloodstained shirt or the murder

weapon. 'No, my *baas*,' a calm and collected parent would lie to the police. 'I'm sure there's been a terrible mistake. My son has been home all evening; he was never out of this house. They must have given you the wrong information, 'strue's God, my *baas*; God can punish me; God is my witness.'

In the ghetto, as in the courtroom, God is always the witness, always the corroborator of whatever lie or truth we choose to give to those we fear or love. Always the witness.

. . .Some secrets are the dark and grotesque thoughts we hide in the tunnels of our minds; to be kept away from the inquisitive eye of the sun; away from those we hate or fear; away from those we love and say we trust. And with the passage of time our souls begin to rot and fall apart.

And sometimes, for the more frequent, smaller, venial misdemeanours, a corrupted policeman would leave a house smiling smugly with several crisp pound notes nestling secretly in his pocket. Police work paid lousy wages in those days. But there were also many upright and deeply moral folks who lived and died by the golden rule. And looking back now, I think perhaps those parents and relations who kept silent were like us, also caged animals — trapped by the same despicable process of dehumanisation. To keep silent was one of several unwritten codes, and it often meant survival.

When my uncle Willie returned home to Sophiatown after the War, he did not have to struggle to find a job like many black — and white — returned soldiers, for my grandfather's bus business guaranteed him the security that the Smuts Government of the day failed to give to the men who had risked their lives fighting the Germans.

The worst affected were the black ex-servicemen: Africans, coloureds and Indians who had come back full of the zeal of victory and bright visions of emancipation for all South Africa's oppressed people. Smuts's promises proved empty; joblessness and poverty quickly blurred those visions and dreams. There were hungry mouths to feed and bodies to clothe and lives to be protected. Victory can be a bad provider. Unemployment and food scarcity resulted in a mass exodus from the rural areas to the cities, and Johannesburg was the hardest-hit of the big towns. Sporadic incidents of petty lawlessness escalated to new and shocking proportions when the criminal elements joined forces to create a vast, sophisticated network. So gripping and violent were the post-War crimes, that many white people believed that the American underworld syndicates had a stake in South African crime.

The gangs grew with every daring exploit of theft, robbery and burglary, perpetrated mainly against the rich. But it was not long before the poor also fell victim. The stronger gangs became brazen in their attacks. One such outfit, the Underworld, had come into existence before the War. My father, known as 'The Don', 'Graaf', 'Don Zinga' or 'Mabanda' was a leading member of this gang. Other members included a former professional heavyweight boxer called Kwembu (Gilbert Moloi), also known as 'The Shot' or 'Bra K'. The Underworld were mostly gambling sharks and conmen who lived by their wits. They ruled the billiard and gambling dens of Sophiatown and a place called Malay Camp, which huddled between the mine shaft complexes of Crown Mines and Langlaagte on the southwestern fringe of Johannesburg. My father's clan consisted of pickpockets, confidence tricksters, dagga pedlars, boxers and musical entertainers. Their leader Boetikies September, also known as 'The Boss', was a seven-foot giant with hands as big as boxing gloves, who hated bullies, especially policemen. According to stories about him — related in the streets and homes of Sophiatown — September used to accost policemen and free people they had arrested. One story had it that he lifted a police vehicle and toppled it over after the driver refused to release a group of prisoners. September's fists were lethal weapons, and he used them mostly for the protection of the weak. 'But there were occasions,' said his younger brother Danie, 'when Boetikies would go berserk and smash everything in his path. People would lie strewn in the streets like puppets cut off from their strings.'

It was during one such mood that he fought a gang of armed 'Russians' — Basotho gangsters — with his bare fists, crushing the skulls of three before being chopped and stabbed to death. The battle had been long and fierce, and so was the vengeance of the Underworld. People spoke about that war for many years to come and Boetikies September became one of the heroic legends of Sophiatown folklore.

There were notorious killers like Mafaago Makhene, and 'Philli-the-Hawk', who murdered his unfaithful wife and pleaded 'guilty on reason' in a dramatic High Court trial. The judge accepted his reasons but jailed him for ten years.

Drie was one of the sharpest pickpockets in Johannesburg: what his thumb, forefinger and middle finger could not remove from a pocket or handbag, his knife would. There was a cripple called 'The Yank' whose knife struck terror in the hearts of young and old alike. Yank, Drie, The Hawk and Mafaago all lived on our property under the protection of my family which was respected by the Underworld.

One of the pre-Second World War gangs that escaped the spotlight of the media and many authors was the Orange and Black, which first began as a coon carnival dance troupe among the tough guys who ruled the northeast end of Sophiatown (between Toby and Willie Streets from the top of Edward Road down to Milner Street). The Orange and Black expanded their territorial conquests until during the War years they came into violent conflict with the Underworld. 'Tollie Hoenderhaan' (The Rooster), leader of the Orange and Black, was captured by Underworld bodybuilder Makoro, and tied naked to the iron railings that divided Western Native Township from Sophiatown. He was stabbed, whipped and humiliated, and so ended the Orange and Black, from whose ashes the dreaded Berliners would rise to crime and infamy.

The 'Mawagraphone', as the Berliners were also called, ruled the former Orange and Black territory, but extended their kingdom beyond Edward Road into the teeming, boiling Victoria Street — gangland's most notorious human cauldron of pimps, prostitutes and politicians, and hoodlum preachers who were angels by day and devils by night.

The Berliners ravaged the areas under their direct control, robbing and raping, and extorting businessmen and taxi owners, and professional people whom they dubbed 'situations' because they preferred to speak English instead of the *tsotsi taal* lingo of the streets. The demise of the Orange and Black also marked the end of the other pre-War criminal masterminds such as the Underworld and 'lone ranger' operators like Mgodoyi who fled Sophiatown to set up a crime network and begin a reign of terror in Alexandra Township.

The Berliners, who numbered about two to three hundred, owned more guns than the local police station, and they used them effectively. Their main gunmen, such as Rex Berlin, 'The Gunfighter', were feared for their cold-bloodedness. They extorted protection money from wealthy Indians and Chinese, and terrorised the population of Western Native Township, until all that township's splinter groups came together to form the Co-operatives Gang, led by a big-headed ugly jail-bird and murderer called Machine-gun. The new gang challenged the Berliners to its detriment, and lost one of its own generals, Potoki, who was killed by the Berliner Black Mamba. The Berliner leader, Vivian, was a cruel sadistic womaniser and convicted murderer, who kicked like a mule. He often kicked his victims, men or women, in their private parts. His gang and the Americans would battle in front of the Odin cinema and carried the bloodshed to the streets, where guns, knives, swords and choppers would settle the day. It was one of the bloodiest and most protracted battles in the history of Sophiatown. Many died. Others were imprisoned. They became the subject of many long arguments, as people recounted their daring, their viciousness and their foolishness. There were lessons to learn.

No story about gangsterism or violence in the townships of Johannesburg can be complete without that of 'Kort Boy' — real name George Mbalweni — the five-foot-nothing knifeman from Benoni, a former mining town on the East Rand, near Johannesburg. The Afrikaans word *kort* means short and 'boy' was characteristic of the many 'Boys' that made up the cream of his gang, the Americans. There was Fat Boy, who was exactly what his name implied, Boy Selengkie, Boy Leelinka and Boy-Boy. All this in turn stemmed from American movie slang and crime novels, which referred to the street-wise city slickers as 'bright boys'. And the USAs, as the gang was also called, had many such bright boys — daring thieves and ruthlessly violent men.

Bra Boy, as Kort Boy was fraternally known to the young prospective street-fighters, was a different man to different people, kind to his friends and admirers and cruel to his enemies — and since he had more of the latter, Bra Boy's reputation was that of a savagely cruel man. Newspapers and magazines such as *Drum* and *High Note* carried sensational monthly articles about his exploits. Crime stories became so popular that the magazines often published follow-up articles giving the historical backgrounds and origins of such gangs as the Americans, the Berliners, the Gestapo and the Co-operatives. Kort Boy was a legend in his day — much hated, much loved — it all depended on which end of his knife you were at.

Fashionable and favourite with the ladies and young boys, the

Americans wore only the best in American clothes. They staged daylight robberies and often exchanged gunfire with the railway police who suffered considerable losses in theft. Ferreira, a cunning Boer railway police officer, formed a special squad to fight the organised thefts by the Americans. He shot and killed Boy-Boy, and in retaliation members of the police were knifed and shot. The police intensified their fight against the Americans. Many gang members were arrested, convicted and jailed for long terms.

The Gestapo were a gang of boxers who had a training centre in Sophiatown's notorious Victoria Street. They were tough hard-knuckled men who used to challenge people indiscriminately in the streets to fist fights, and always ended up winning. The Gestapo inevitably came into conflict with the Berliners and with the Americans, and later turned to robbery and protection fee racket-eering against Indian shopkeepers.

The Americans had a gunman called Chanaam, alias The Durango Kid, a successful womaniser who always carried two guns and had the reputation of being the fastest gun alive. Through his efforts, the Gestapo dissolved overnight. They scattered into Western and Newclare and deeper into Pimville and Moroka Jabavu — to give birth to other outfits such as the Torch Gang and the dreaded Peter Nchechane Gang of White City Jabavu whose two top men, Boy Sevenpence and Maboy, had shared a prison cell with me in 1955 when we all faced different murder charges. As they said in the business: the death of one gang was the birth of others.

Kort Boy murdered a rival gang member and was sentenced to death, but his sentence was commuted to eighteen years' hard labour. This was after he had served a short jail term for the killing of a school principal, and after being acquitted of a knifing during a dice game. He served fifteen years and returned to find his Kofifi razed to the ground. Most of his gang members were jailed for long terms; others had died or were on their way to the grave. Time had caught up with him as it had for many of Sophiatown's bright boys — including me and members of our gang. The Durango Kid submitted to the whims and demands of changing times. He died a sick and lonely man.

There are only a handful of American gang members left. Kort Boy is one of them. . . .

The year is 1985, and Kort Boy can usually be seen walking up and down the same streets of Johannesburg city that he and his thieving Americans used to raid with impunity. He works as a messenger for a commercial company; his once proud and stubborn shoulders are now bent and subdued. And although his eyes have dimmed with the passage of the years, I always see a hidden fire and history in them of which I was once both hunter and prey. Whenever we meet the glow of a fraternal and remembered familiarity warms us to the point of evoking a deep nostalgia for what was yesterday; what was Sophiatown; what was his teeming, colourful and violent past and my own youthful and adventurous delinquency.

That he had killed, that I had killed, will remain an eternal indictment against us. But it is an indictment which society of that time as well as of today must share.

Slowly, perhaps unconsciously and because of my boxing ability, early in 1951 I became caught in the snare of violence. I led the Vultures which crushed and took over other smaller outfits like the Congo Kids, Black Raiders, Styles and the Young Berliners. Ours became the most powerful teenage gang in Sophiatown and neighbouring Western. Our membership spiralled with every conquest. amd we fought police and rivals with equal audacity stabbing, shooting and even killing. Young Robin Hoods, fighting the strong in defence of the weak, or so I would like it to have been, because most of the battles were not started by me. It was mostly some big guy, who needed to be taught a lesson because he'd beaten up a smaller boy.

I remember how some nights a shrill, familiar whistle would awaken me: a call to arms. Sometimes I returned home, my hands and clothes bloodstained; my head or face cut by stone and glass; my body scarred and stabbed and singed by a police bullet or a rival knife. My name spread like wildfire across the streets and alleys of Sophiatown in songs and curses. Many vowed that my mother would find me dead in the passages of the slum, and rivals whose parents believed in or practised black magic often promised that my hands would be crippled, and that I would walk the streets picking up papers like a madman. They may not have succeeded in twisting my limbs, but in a strange way my mind had gradually moved towards a twisted death-wish.

My father tried every method of persuasion, from talking to violence, and even barred me from his house. My other paternal relatives did not seem to care what became of me. They were only thankful for my name and the general respect I procured for them through my exploits. The rest was my own affair, they said. I was becoming a man. But not the man my father wanted me to become. He didn't say it, but deep inside I knew that I had failed him.

Kehtie, a Young Berliner I'd hammered in a tough fist fight, joined our ranks together with some of his gang. He was the younger brother of Rex-Gunfighter of the Berliner gang. Word had gone around that Vivian the notorious, their leader, had been released from jail where he had served some time for murder. Things were going to change. There were too many young bosses about for his liking and he had returned to restore the fading glory of the old Sophiatown gangland.

Then one day it happened. Kehtie grabbed Vivian's beautiful half-Indian, half-African woman as she passed Gibson Street.

'Where's the Mule?' he asked her. She didn't say a word. Then he grabbed her breasts and repeated the question. Vivian the Mule appeared suddenly and without warning kicked Kehtie in the stomach.

That was enough. I attacked Vivian and he fell. Kehtie kicked at him and opened his knife, but I stopped him.

'One day I'm going to kill this dog. One day, so help me, this mother's arse is going to die,' Kehtie swore as we dragged him away from the half-dazed Mule.

Kehtie lived to fulfil that threat. He waylaid the unsuspecting Vivian near a bus-stop in the city. The ambulance carried away the Mule from the platform of a bus. There were numerous stab wounds that helped to convict Kehtie and sentence him to a term of eighteen years in prison. The only extenuating circumstance the judge found was Vivian's long life of crime — which included murder: he was a twice-convicted killer. Turkas, who had given Kehtie the knife, was sentenced to twelve years in a maximum security prison.

One cold Monday morning at the bus-stop, a schoolmate called Norman Edwards handed me his schoolbag. He told me he would be coming in late to school.

Aboo, a young Indian fellow, approached me with his hand in his coat pocket. Now hands in pockets don't augur well in the gangster game. Aboo wanted the five pounds I had extorted from his younger brother for services rendered.

The school bus stopped in front of Kanson's at the corner of Good and Victoria Streets. The children got in and I picked up Norman's bag and passed Aboo and three Africans who were with him. One of them pushed me back and asked if I was deaf. I replied yes and he tried to hit me, but my blade sagged into his flesh and blood spurted onto my shirt. He called for Aboo who brandished a Browning pistol and aimed at my stomach.

Instinctively I lifted the bag, and felt a thud against it. Aboo lifted his aim and another bullet whizzed past me to hit the shop window, making a neat hole. Then the gun jammed and as I rushed at him, I felt a burning sensation in my thigh. A bullet penetrated the bone and found an exit below my left buttock. I began running but Aboo meant business. He fired at me for the fourth time and jumped over a fence. He came fuming and fired two more shots. By this time, my shoes were full of blood.

Some Indian friend told me that Aboo's people were rich and that if I wanted money they would pay. Aboo's mediator, Harry, came to our home.

'No dropping the case. Money for blood. Blood for money,' my father told Harry.

But Harry offered twenty pounds. I demanded fifty. My dad nodded from his corner. Harry didn't see him. Then the auctioneering began:

'Thirty,' Harry said sternly, authority in his voice. Wasn't he dealing with a boy?

Aboo, Harry said, was a student teacher. Conviction would ruin his chances of graduating and then moving on to something better. We had to talk the whole thing over like friends. He knew my father and my father knew him. It was in the family, you might say, blood, bullets and money. My blood. Their bullets. Our money. Aboo and I were just children and this serious mistake could be settled out of court.

I stuck firmly to fifty. Harry looked pleadingly at my father, but the old man shrugged and said, 'His blood Harry, his money.'

Disappointed, Harry shouted: 'Thirty-five. Take it or leave it.' He turned to watch my father.

I cleared my throat and tried to speak, but only a croaking sound came out. Harry smiled triumphantly; he had heard the noise before — as when the towel is being thrown in.

But a surprise 'Fifty!' hit Harry square in the face. He moved to forty, then forty-five and wiped his brow.

'Your son is in the wrong business,' he told my father in defeat. 'He strikes a heavy bargain.' As the fifty crisp pound notes nestled in my palm, I was ordered by my father to buy 'Uncle Harry' something, meaning liquor. The deal was clinched. I was happy and Aboo graduated. . . .

A new gang in Western Native Township, the Headquarters — led by Chops Number Five and strengthened by the Pirates and Spoilers of Newclare — badly injured one of my boys. It was a challenge they were to regret for a long time. The Headquarters ruled parts of Western and had the sympathy of the adult Co-operatives Gang. Open gang clashes on the football field and dusty streets made daily newspaper headlines. I carried a Browning pistol and often fired it without concern that someone could be killed or injured. We never thought of death; only of making names for ourselves.

One November day, the 'blackjacks' (municipal police) of Western arrested Dudley Badenhorst, one of the many coloured boys in my gang. He was handcuffed and beaten with sticks and as he was being dragged to the municipal office, a woman poured boiling water on him. He was also stabbed in the head and back. In vengeance, we converged on the office of the blackjacks. We freed Dudley.

The South African Police, in two squad cars, raced through the streets and before they could jump out, we attacked. I fired several shots. It happened so fast, they were stunned into immobility. The Vultures made for the narrow alleys. A police bullet ripped my calf. Another hit a pine tree as I passed. Nana, one of my fearless men, fell to the ground.

A bullet had pierced his left shoulder. I managed to drag him into a yard. We took refuge in a lavatory. I left him there and hit the road. That night I did not go home, nor did I go to school the next day. We decided that November 19 would be the night of our vengeance. Our disguise would be working overalls and balaclava caps; our faces smeared with polish; no names to be mentioned but those of rival gang members. Weapons of all sorts and sizes would be used, including guns. I was to lead the pre-midnight attack and no quarter would be given.

November 19 came. The steeple clock at Westdene chimed the midnight hour. Twenty-two Vultures, heavily disguised, moved through the night, smashing street lights. The first victim was Moolato, a member of the FGs which had affiliated to the Headquarters. He did not know what hit him and was left crawling in the sand and holding onto his stomach.

'Leave the dog, Mfanzeni,' shouted Max, addressing Tolla-Tolla by a rival gang member's name.

Several members of the Headquarters were dancing with girls around a fire. They sang about their victory over Dudley, Skrewdriver and Nana. One of them said goodnight to his friends.

'Don't let the Vultures eat you up,' someone called, unaware that we were waiting in a nearby alley. The words had hardly died down when Shakes, acting as if he were drunk, pounced on the unwary victim. His cries for help were muffled. Knives, choppers, bayonets sagged into his white dust-coat and he called for his mother.

I shot into the unsuspecting fire-dancers and heard a cry of pain. It was from Mabuto, a Headquarters chief, who I had hit in the hip. We surrounded them and attacked from all angles, calling each other by false names. Doors and windows opened; lights flashed. Someone shouted, 'It's the Berlins! The Berlins are killing our boys!' Police whistles rang out to alert the township of the midnight terror. All twenty-two of us vanished and made for home.

On December 19 1955, a Monday morning, the postman brought my school report which said I had passed to standard nine. A few hours later, several police squad cars pulled up in front of my father's house.

A police special six-shooter pressed deep into my ribs; had it been a sharp instrument it would have drawn blood. Its owner, an unsmiling and scruffy Afrikaner sergeant called Klopper, stood about seven feet tall. In Newclare he was known as 'Klopper the Vicious' because of his violent temper and his no-nonsense attitude when it came to enforcing 'his law' against the Basotho 'Russians' clan that ruled the area with an equally vicious iron hand. Klopper was the kind of policeman some people believed came from the fabled comic-strip city of Krypton because of his almost superhuman strength and brute force. Klopper the Vicious was also a crack shot with a rifle or revolver. Nobody, but nobody, as far as I can recall, ever dared to run away from him; in fact Klopper's pass raid victims were never handcuffed but were made to hold hands and to walk in pairs. There were also rumours going that he had once told ten pairs of pass law 'offenders' to go on ahead to the police station because he was going home for a bite. Word had it that he warned them against escaping: 'I've taken a mental photograph of each one of you, so watch out. I want to see all twenty of you when I get to the station.' The un-bangled couples had sheepishly nodded their heads and all but one couple had reported to the station exactly as Klopper had ordered.

The Vicious interrogated me. I had no trouble persuading myself to answer all questions with alacrity. 'Are you Don Mattera, other-wise known as *ou* Zinga, boss of the Vultures?' I nodded.

'Did you and your boys kill that student in Western Native Township?' I hesitated for what seemed to be almost a hundred years. I shook my head.

'Can't you open your blerry mouth? Nobody nods or shakes his head at me, *Hotnot*. Did you *moerskonts* (motherfuckers) kill that *fokken* kaffir last month?' I shook my head but for the last time, because a crushing blow sent me sprawling and spitting blood. The same fluid trickled from my nose and vanished into my jersey. The two African detectives also had a field day on me. I lay on the ground, stunned and very dizzy. They searched our house. Question-ed about a firearm, I told them I didn't even know what a firearm looked like, at which Klopper sniggered and landed another blow on my chest.

I coughed and fought for air. . . .

10. Jail

The cell was dark and as the warder pushed me into it, I stumbled over a fellow prisoner. He groaned and cursed. I felt a blow against my ear. Angered and in pain, I held on to him; feeling for his face. I hit him hard. The man screamed and broke free. I sat and bundled myself up, my body still aching from the police blows.

The next morning, and to my shame, I saw the man huddled in a lonely corner of the cell, his grey hair dyed red with blood from the deep gash I had inflicted on his cheek. 'God, what have I done to you, old man?' I called out to him.

But he covered his head and screamed: 'Please don't hit me. Somebody please stop him. Don't let him hurt me again.'

I felt so remorseful and ashamed; the man was older than my father. What a bad start to a new life; beating up an old man; what would people outside think of me? Later that afternoon I tried to repair the damage. I spoke to him and apologised and having done that, I won myself a friend who would help and advise me during bad times. There were about thirty of us in the thirty foot square prison cell — some of them rival gang members like Seawater of Headquarters and Gobee and Sesse of the Pirates gang, whose stab-and-run tactics had made fighting against them a most tiring exercise until we used decoys to trap and ambush them. Would the battle be pursued in the cell? I was alone against three and I prepared myself for a fight. Instead they greeted me with respect and called me over to share their food. They faced individual charges of attempted murder, robbery and rape, and these did not appear to bother them. Just routine; just business. We talked and recalled with twisted humour our exploits of violence and delinquent fun which had left one dead and many, many injured. Nobody among us dared to ask why we chased and fought and killed one another; to ask would have revealed a streak of yellow. Being afraid and running was forgiveable, but cowardice was different. And so, Seawater, Gobee and Sesse broke bread with me. For that night at least, and while prison bars joined us ironically in friendship, we spoke together and laughed. But the time would come when the fever of fratricide would infect us and the warm comradeship we had known in jail would be forgotten.

The time would come. . . .

I saw one man bend over to kiss another; his hand fondled his 'lover' between the legs. When darkness came, they would find each other like so many others did. In one corner near the urine and waste bucket, a coloured sang his freedom song: 'Show me the way to go home/I'm tired an' I wanna go to bed. . . .' Home. It seemed a long, long time since I had been there. Home is where the heart is, but my heart wasn't anywhere; wasn't feeling, wasn't longing. . . .

A short, stocky, bandy-legged man kept looking at my legs. I was wearing shorts and a maroon jersey. The police had refused me permission to dress properly. The stocky guy whom everyone appeared to know kept smiling. I walked up to him and asked if he liked what he saw. The man they called Kid Dash nodded: 'I want you to be my woman tonight. . . .' His words were smothered in his mouth. I pounded him so viciously that the warders had to hit me on the head to stop me. Newlands police station was *my* territory and nobody was going to make me his woman. Kid Dash was taken to the prison infirmary. He warned me that vengeance would be his at Number Four prison — also called the Johannesburg Fort. It was only a matter of time.

Outside in the street, across the main road and in Sophiatown, people were starting their Christmas Day. All the familiar sounds and the noise; the eating and drinking; the festivities and the frolicking permeated the cell. Dark faces, broken and battered by crime and the pains of dispossession, lit up to catch the Christmas revelry. Dark faces in the semi-darkness of our cell responded mechanically like the man who masturbated in his quiet corner; his eyes scanning the cell to see who was watching him.

'Show me the way to go home. . .' rang the plaintive, pleading voice, 'show me the way to go home. . . .'

Christmas in prison; no moving carols no good wishes and worst of all, no relatives or friends. A young and round-faced girl, Winnie, who sold food, fruit and sweets at a bus stop in Western, brought me my favourite peppermint sweets, a jam doughnut and a pint of milk. Because I was popular at the time among young girls, Winnie had chosen me to be her 'daddy'. Every tough guy had one or more 'babies'. My eyes widened and I took a ring from my small finger and gave it to her.

Small gifts for a man in a cage, with its dirty stinking blankets, urine buckets that overflowed, and lice that sucked all joy and hope from the wounded flesh and the hardened heart. That night a man went beserk and holding a tin dish in his hand, he hit at us wildly and tried to grab the wire meshed windows. We pounced on him and pinned him down. A Boer warder came into the cell and kicked him in the stomach while we held him down. We laughed. Someone shouted: *'Die hond is befok, my baas!'* (the dog's gone mad, my *baas!)* We all burst out laughing as the man groaned and shook. His pain was real; our laughter was not. It was fawning and self-deprecating to show the *'baas'* that we were 'good kaffirs' and 'good Bushmen', who knew their places. *'Skop die hond, my kroon, hy's lekker befok.'* (kick the dog, my crown, he's nice and mad.)

Christmas in prison. . . .

The old man with blood in his hair called out to me. I crossed over on my knees; still remorseful and contrite for the beating I'd given him. 'Happy *Krismis,'* he said, pushing his hand into mine. *'Mag die*

Here jou seën en spaar!' (May God bless and keep you!) I held his hand firmly and found myself in his arms, my head against his soft, ageing body. 'Happy *Krismis* daddy,' I said with a croak in my voice. The urine bucket singer shouted *'Heppie! Heppie! O Here God, heppie.'* — (Happy! Happy! O Lord God, happy!) That was the shortest Christmas carol I had ever heard. It warmed me inside and sparked a tiny longing for my dear mother. She of all my relatives would at least remember my twentieth birthday — four days after Christmas.

From a nearby cell we heard the madman scream for his mother, and for God and for the man whose birthday the world was celebrating. He screamed so many times that I shuddered. The lights were put out and from where I lay, I pictured the little African girl in the bright red dress with matching shoes, standing in the visitors' queue with her three tiny gifts for me. A deep peace and joy filled my heart. 'Show me the way to go home/I'm tired an' I wanna go to bed. . . .'

When Boxing Day opened its eyes, it found us already awake and on our feet in rows of four, to be counted several times over. 'Two missing; two bastards missing, Khumalo!' the white warder shouted in Afrikaans to his black colleague. 'Yes two, my *baas*. The madman is in that single cell outside and the other one that was beaten by the Bushman' — he pointed at me — 'is in the prison clinic.'

'Which Bushman hit him?'

'That one, *basie;* the one in short pants.'

'So you're the one that fucked up Kid Dash eh?'

I nodded.

'Then you're in for shit. His people rule Number Four and since you are such a strong *Hotnot,* I'm sending you there in three days' time,' the *'basie'* said. That would be Thursday, my birthday. During a previous arrest I was held awaiting trial at Marshall Square police station in the city. I had also spent Christmas there. The things people said about Number Four chilled the blood and yet strangely I was filled with a sense of bravado and expectancy. There was nothing in the world that scared me. Come Thursday I was going to prove it. . . .

The counting done, we were 'set free' from the cells and stamped-ed into the large courtyard for the traditional breakfast of half-cooked maize porridge, brown bread called *'katkop'* (cat's head) and sugarless black coffee. The inmates rushed like starving pigs. I saw my old friend fall and helped him to his feet. He laughed and pointed to the food. I pushed through and returned with his breakfast. He smiled and patted me gently on the head: *'Dankie, my laaitie.'* (Thank you, my son.) I sat next to him; he ate voraciously for an old man and without looking up. His brakfast vanished in a couple of minutes. I gave him mine which he also devoured in a few moments; gone. I could not understand how such an old man could eat so much, so fast. He broke wind, then asked if I smoked. I shook my head and called Seawater who provided him with a long cigarette.

'Your Christmas box, old timer. They're expensive and hard to come by in here.' Seawater was not exaggerating the scarcity nor the expensiveness of cigarettes in prison. Most prisoners smoked tobacco rolled in paper known as a *'zol'* which was passed around in a circle of friends. Other inmates sold their backsides for a packet of cigarettes or a bar of chocolate.

The old man asked me what my name was and what charge I was facing. I told him. He nodded several times and put his hand on my shoulder and said murder was a serious charge. He said nothing about it being a serious act; for in jail the first consideration was the charge and not the life that had been taken, nor the victim whose house or shop had been burgled; nor the girl or woman raped. No-one gave a thought to the terror or the trauma of being raped. During those days the accused or the convict was always the aggrieved, always the victim.

'My son, are your folks going to get you a lawyer? These days the 'jits' (judges) take very unkindly to murder, especially jits like Maritz, Ludorf and Steyn. People call them the hanging jits.'

'How do you know these things, dad?'

'Because I've been around, my son; I've been around so long some folks think I'm a piece of the furniture.'

When you say you've been around are you telling me that you have been in prison before?'

'Ja, many times; more than you have had birthdays.' When I tried to probe further the old man put his hand on my shoulder, pushed himself up and walked away.

'Daddy, what is your name?' He turned around, smiled and gave a spritely hop to one side. As if addressing a huge audience, he declaimed: 'Pietersen; my name is Isaak Pietersen!' He melted into a crowd of elderly men who were smoking long tobacco *zols* and telling dirty jokes. A siren bundled us into rows of four to be counted according to our cell numbers. We were marched to our cell in fours and re-counted as we entered it. The heavy steel doors banged shut. The rattling keys sealed us off from a society that always wanted its pound of flesh and always got it. Among the ten new arrivals that were pushed into our cell were four junior members of our gang — Maasanto, Churchill, Deadline and Tolla-Tolla. They had all participated in that fateful night of human butchery, and ran happily towards me, their leader. Deadline and Churchill, young and pigheaded at the worst and best of times, recognised Gobee, Sesse and Seawater.

'What the fucking hell are these dogs doing here? Hey you Headquarters and Pirates *'bangies'* (cowards), why do you dogs like to stab-and-run?' teased Churchill.

'*Ja,*' said Deadline. 'You dogs never stand your ground; always bloody running. Your bra couldn't run the other night. We had him trapped. He screamed for his mother!' I moved between them and the rival trio and urged my boys to accept them. 'They've been good to me and nobody is going to hurt them while I'm around,' I said with finality. But Churchill couldn't resist a last jibe: 'And if we do get out, don't even greet me because I may stab you.' Seawater, who was my age, shook his head and walked away to the farthest corner of the cell. The boys and I talked past the time the lights were switched off and into the early morning. They said the fighting had stopped after my arrest and the police were hunting for more of our gang — many of whom were hiding in Sophiatown or had fled Johannesburg.

'Bra Zinga, things are really bad. The cops are raiding every house. There's a girl moving around with them; she's pointing out the houses,' said Maasanto the faithful, who was very close to my heart and blindly dedicated to me. I could say to him: 'Kill that man. Get me that girl. Rob that shop,' and he would obey. But Maasanto and Deadline would one day clash, and standing up for Maasanto would earn me a bullet in my back. My gang was in a shambles. The outfit that had begun as a small defender of the young and the weak was being hounded for the bunch of killers it had become. The boys felt important and appeared to be unconcerned about the future, about their lives or about the 'hanging jits' that old Pietersen had

ːd about. And I was partly to blame. But that night I did not think about it; nor did they.

When Thursday came, our ways parted. The four Vultures were taken by a long police escort vehicle to a 'place of safety' — a reformatory — until the day of our joint appearance. Seawater, Sesse and Gobee remained at Newlands, and winked at me as I got into the huge vehicle, the last of eighty awaiting trial prisoners; one of them old Pietersen.

I remembered the *'basie's'* threat: 'Your're in for shit; Kid Dash's people rule Number Four!' I had always believed that the white government ruled the country and especially the jails. Jail was a form of government, a state within a state, and Kid Dash, the stocky short man who had wanted to sleep with me, was one of the rulers of the country called Number Four. A cold terror stood beside me in that steel truck with the six round ventilation openings when the Kid stared at me. He placed his thumb between his first and second fingers in a sexual intimation. I moved closer and pressed my fist into his mouth: 'Anytime, any place; I'll be ready for you, you short bastard. Anytime dammit!' Some of the co-riders goaded me on. 'Fuck him up,' they shouted, *'moer* him!' But I let it ride. The heavy-duty vehicle rolled out of the yard at deliberate tortoise speed as if to say: 'Have a last look; next stop Number Four.'

My mind went back to November 11 and our attack on Headquarters territory in Western, when I had shot at a blackjack and seen him fall. Two others with him ran for safety. Blackjack reinforcements arrived and I shot at them wildly and emptied the gun. I ran out of the township and headed for the flat complex where the coloured ex-servicemen lived. Police whistles awoke several families as members of my gang ran for safety and I was on my own, running, panting, praying. I hid underneath a car crouched between the two front wheels. The blackjacks, who were assisted by several rival gang members, ran past me. I crawled out and ran towards an opening but a man who was hiding in the shadows hit me on the head. I heard him shout: I've got him! I've got him!' The pursuers returned. Stick blows and whip lashes rained on me and I was stabbed four inches into my left lung. Someone threw water over my head. The boy who had stabbed me jumped around in front of me, dancing and shouting jubilantly.

I could not breathe and asked for water. A woman threw water in my face. After what seemed like a dream, we arrived at the township offices where my captors threw me to the floor. I asked for water and the blackjack I had earlier shot at kicked me in the face and then gave me water from the lid of a Vaseline jar. An ambulance arrived. I shall never forget their deliberate delaying tactics in getting me inside the vehicle. So many slow-motion moments elapsed, and I saw many happy, smiling faces fade as I was lifted into the ambulance. Someone shouted in Zulu: 'The dog is strong; so many wounds and so much blood, and he is still alive. This *Boesman* is strong!' Coronation Hospital was only a short drive from the township but it seemed like an hour before we entered the casualty section and I was admitted.

One day after my admission, I was still full of transfusion tubes when three members of the Headquarters attacked and stabbed me under the right arm, and cut the tubes. Nurses and hospital orderlies rescued me. The boy whose knife had pierced my lung the day before was one of the assailants.

He paid with his life. The same life I would be answering for in court. The same life which Kid Dash and his people would make me regret I took.

'Show me the way to go home. . . .'

The police vehicle passed familiar territory: many Indian shops whose owners' sons used to donate money towards our gang's coffers for the purchase of guns and knives. Some people called it protection fees; we saw it as important business transactions. The truck moved closer to Good Street — the scene of much of Sophiatown's violence and killing, hardly a good street. Then Papagees's fruit shop where we played a ballbearing game of chance to win or lose our bioscope seats. Past the bottom of Gerty Street — my street — with Goldberg's chemist as its sentry and tollgate. It was also the meeting place for our gang because it served as both entrance and exit to Western Native Township and the surrounding townships. There were no passages or short cuts into our street from the south.

As the police vehicle dragged itself down our street I thought fleetingly about what the folks at home would be doing; what my cousin Chossie and my five-year-old half-brother Pasquale were up to. It was Thursday — my father's day off from the buses where he worked as an inspector. I wondered whether he had remembered my birthday.

Goodbye Gerty Street; hello Number Four. From the corner of his fat eye, the Kid looked at me furtively. A glint of impending vengeance brighter than the morning star showed in his smug face.

Number Four. Kid Dash's unofficial government waited for us more eagerly than I had imagined. We were pushed out of the big truck. A fat rhinoceros of an Afrikaner policeman with a permanent froth at the corners of his mouth punched us as we passed him. It was his way of counting us and making sure we were introduced properly. The man's punches were heavy and many of the chaps fell down. I stumbled onto another Boer called Vossie. He kicked at my private parts but I pushed his foot aside. The Kid went up to him. They moved to one side. I saw him point at me; Vossie laughed, then spat. 'Blade,' he called. 'Here is the woman of your dreams. The one who hit your kid brother.' He pointed to my backside and to the short pants sitting tightly on my well-developed thighs — the result of boxing and dumb-bell exercises. Blade smiled and kissed my cheek. *'Bushie-meid,'* (Bushman-girl) he said to the joy of the two Boers and Kid Dash. I pushed him and he landed on the cement floor.

Blade got up and punched me. He was off the mark. I hit him hard. He fell and lay still. A baton smacked my head and I lost consciousness. The Kid's government was in control. I was revived and stripped of all my clothes. Other men, grown and ugly, were playing with my penis and backside. Blade was about to mount me when I summoned every ounce of strength in my body, and in a rage of near insanity I hit the man so hard that he crashed his head against the admission desk. I screamed and attacked, pounding madly at everyone who stood in my path. The chief warder, a tall and striking Boer called Hoffman entered the reception office. *'Wat die fokken hel gaan hier aan!'* (What the fucking hell is going on here!) he shouted. Another blow felled me. I awoke in the 'koolkoots' a cooling-off cell, stark naked, my badly torn clothes next to me.

Three days later in the early morning, I was taken out of the koolkoots and made to stand with the others, to be counted in rows of four and told to 'washup'. The word attained new dimensions, because 'washup' actually meant dabbing your face and then moving off before Vossie or Smuttie's baton beat you to the ground. Besides, there were Blade and his boys, watching my every move. They were hardened prisoners, serving time. I was only awaiting trial.

A mean looking man, his eyes red and bloodshot, stared at me. I stared back and he called me but I refused to go. He approached me and said in Zulu: 'You look at King Kong and don't come when King Kong calls you, eh?' Before I could answer I lay sprawled against the wall, my mouth bleeding from a cut inside. The King's boot found a soft spot in my stomach and vomit cheated me of the morning's raw porridge and yellow fat, the piece of hard bread and the black weak coffee.

Mamba, a feared Sophiatown hood, who belonged to the adult Berliners and was charged with murder, saved me from further beating when he told the King I was one of his boys. King nodded lazily and warned that I should never look at him again, or it would be worse the next time. I did not argue — besides there was no breath left in me. And who in his right mind would exchange words or even looks with the woman killer. A strange thing happened, though. Pietersen who had watched the assault on me, and did not intervene, approached King Kong and spoke to him privately. Thereafter the King, whose real name was Ezekiel Dlamini, treated me like one of his own family.

But Blade and the Kid were not satisfied with the state of affairs and had hoped that King Kong would finish the job for them. Mamba the Sophiatown strongman had further complicated their plans. And so, the 'government' planned to get rid of me and Zorro the killer from Alexandra Township would do the job.

'Don, Mr Fick wants you in his classroom; something to do with the English recitation for the Eisteddfod.' The speaker was a standard eight classmate, Calvin Julius, a long standing friend from primary school days. Cyril Fick was an arithmetic teacher who knew my father, and whose own parents had once lived in our street. I entered his classroom with slight trepidation; only he gave me lectures about my bad conduct and at times punished me without fear of being accosted by my gang — unlike some of my other teachers.

'Sir, I understand you want to see me?'

'Yes. I hear you have been shot again.'

'Again, Mr Fick?'

'Twice in one weekend to be precise, Mr Mattera. Last time some-one stabbed you in the arm; then in your head. Just two weeks ago, before the Easter holidays, you fought on the school grounds; then in the toilet with Mukkadam's son. God, when will you listen? When you're dead or crippled?'

'Mukkadam called me a kaffir, sir, and ever since I came to this school in 1953, he's been picking fights and saying bad things about me. Sir, I don't like to fight but when someone calls me a kaffir well I. . . .'

'Just listen to that. . . that violent talk; God, what does your father or your family say about your conduct? Do they speak to you?'

'Nobody says anything; nobody cares!'

'Not even your mother?'

'No, sir. . . .'

'I don't believe that. . . .'

'Sir, you can believe what you want, but I'm telling you nobody cares.'

'What about the Eisteddfod? Mr Gordon wants to know whether you are going to participate. He says you stand a good chance of bringing in a gold for our school. Will you take part? Listen I'm tell-ing you, no, I'm ordering you to take part.'

'Ordering me, sir?'

'Yes! And that's final.'

I looked at him and smiled. There was an important silence bet-ween us; between his strong eyes and compassionate mouth, and the burning inside of me, that preferred argument and confrontation above compassion and understanding.

'Sir! I don't have a school uniform nor a blazer; what must I wear?'

'Dress up like a Chinaman if you can — besides Somerset Maugham might be in the audience to hear how you recite "On a Chinese Screen".'

I took the gold medal along with a citation for the best ever, most authentic performance of the poem in the history of its presentation nationally. I became a hero for the right reason and it made me feel good. I took the medal and citation home but I did not show them to anybody. That night, a shrill whistle sounded from the street. I awoke, dressed and took my ex-soldier uncle's jagged bayonet and crossed the street to lead an attack against the Black Devils and Wibsey Kids in the northern section of Sophiatown.

The citation and the medal — and the glory that came with them — became particles of the dust made by our running, delinquent feet as we chased our enemies into the night. And I returned home, my clothes and hands stained with the blood of another family's sons. . . .

Zorro who was nine years my senior cornered me in the washroom of the A-section; the murderers' row where I slept in a small cell separated from the theft, rape and robbery suspects. His thin, wiry frame stood in front of me as I prepared to leave the lavatory. His shrill, almost shrieky voice had a coldness in it which reminded me of a Count Dracula movie.

'So you are the swankie that whipped Kid Dash and Blade eh?' I ignored him and tried to push my way past. But he pushed me into the toilet.

'Look big man, I've come to listen to my case and not fight with you or Blade or the Kid, so please let me pass.' My voice was stronger now and less afraid.

'Do you know who I am?' I told him I didn't know and didn't want to know.

He told me his name and added: 'Have you heard of me?' I replied in the affirmative, at which he asked where I came from and what charge I faced. When informed, he moved aside and said: 'So you are Don Zinga, *die harde Bushie* (the hardnut Bushman).' I nodded.

'My real name in Changkie; Changkie Mahangwe. And I come from Alexandra Township; also known as the dark city. The people have asked me to teach you a lesson for that beating you gave Blade.' He showed me a spoon which had been sharpened at both ends.

'See this, I can kill you where you stand; just say "otch" (colloquial for 'just dare me'). I don't have a quarrel with you, sonny but the people think you ought to bleed,' said Zorro pointing the home-made weapon at my throat. I felt a strange unwillingness to fight or beg, so I said: 'Bra Zorro I have no fight with you but if you want my blood then take it!' I watched his hands and eyes. A voice behind him said: 'Zet, leave the boy alone; he's with me.' Zorro turned around to face Mamba and old man Pietersen at the two washroom doors. Zorro laughed, then patted my cheeks. 'I was only joking with him bra Isaak; you didn't have to call Mamba. I was only playing.' He moved towards the doorway.

'You want to fight him, Donny?' asked my 'adopted' father.

'I don't have a grouse against him but if he wants to, well then it's okay by me.' My voice was even stronger than I had imagined. Courage was too lean a word to describe the stoutness of heart that old Pietersen and Mamba had helped me to display. I knew that Zorro had in fact come to kill me as the 'government' of Kid Dash, Blade and the Boer warders had gazetted in the invisible code of prison conduct. For if a 'governor' decreed that prisoner so-and-so would be the '*wyfie*' (woman) of one of them, then that would be the 'law'. If the sentence was death by knife or by strangulation it would be executed without question. And in my case, Mamba and the wise old Pietersen had merely stalled or suspended the execution. I knew that it was only a matter of time and the 'state' would assign a new killer.

Zorro — 'Zet' — had the same criminal beginnings as many other township kids; the quiet greenhorn who fights a bully but ends up being one. The man they called 'the terror of Alexandra' had unleashed a scourge of violence on men and women alike. The former he would selectively stab at the base of the spine with a thin spike called *ntshumentshu*. Women who rejected him would be raped, and then the letter 'Z' would be carved on their foreheads. No-one had dared to have him arrested because his criminal web extended to the city of Johannesburg's Noord Street bus terminus where his gang operated a protection fee racket. In the dark city itself several murders were blamed on Zorro and his men and as usual, no witnesses came forward. But with the birth of organised crime in the township under the cloak of the Spoilers and their rivals the Msomis, events overtook Zorro. People grew tired of his bullying and assaults and laid charges against him. He was serving a combined jail sentence of twenty years at the time of my altercation with his 'government'.

I knew that I had to be on my guard all the time, and not eat anything anyone gave me because poison was also one of the methods the 'state' employed in the elimination of its foes. It was something Pietersen had warned me against: '*Vreet en vrek,*' (eat and die) he would say to me. I asked Mamba who Pietersen really was and why so many prisoners and warders showed him so much respect.

'Bra Isaak is an original founder and commander-in-chief of the 'Big 28' convict warlords who rule most of the jails in South Africa. He has been in and out of prison for the last forty-five years as well as spending four years in a reformatory,' said Mamba, who was also on a murder charge, for the killing of Potoki, Co-operatives gang chief of Western Native Township butchered at a dice game in Sophiatown. Mamba was feared by many in our township. Big men with big names used to pay protection fees to Mamba La Gusha as we streetfighters called him. When he spoke about the old man it was with a deep-seated reverence. He and Pietersen used to laugh a lot and had always stuck together in jail. Their *'taal'*, their lingo, contained certain spiritual and physical intimacies that made me feel good and secure in their company.

Mamba, who was acquitted of Potoki's killing, died by the same hand that had helped him in that murder. A circle of vice. Pietersen was facing a charge of murdering an old white pensioner after raping her. It was his third murder charge — and the last he would ever face. He was hanged in 1956 along with more than a hundred other gangsters.

It was old man Pietersen who had told me that jail was not home. Men made women of other men; gave each other good times, good meals and good loving. Those who refused were denied privileges and visits from relatives and friends. Even the two Boer male warders had black male lovers. The murder-rape-robbery row where I slept was occupied mainly by Sophiatowners and hoods from Vrededorp. It was the boxing arena, court-house and gambling den of the A-section single cells. We were not allowed to share cells with the common, petty criminals awaiting the outcome of their cases.

I heard some men speak about the mistakes they had made in trusting women; everyone seemed to have something against women. Inmates briefed each other about the circumstances of their individual charges. There was a 'judge', a 'jury' and 'counsel' for the state and the defence who acted out court scenes with all their inherent drama. The judge was my old Pietersen. He told me that I would win my case; that on the murder charge I would be released, because my alibi was firm and indisputable. The attempted murder charge would be difficult. The only hope would be to 'buy' the complainant who would no doubt, he assured me, be needing extra money.

Isaak Pietersen openly displayed such love and concern for me that many inmates and white warders actually believed I was his own flesh and blood. I came to know him intimately, as if we had lived together for many years, members of the same stricken and cursed family. The two months I shared with him at the 'state' of Number Four, under a sentence of death, opened my eyes. His sadness, his joy and his passion were no longer secrets to me. I understood his fears and pain as if they were mine. I had received profound human fellowship from hands that had murdered three times.

On the final day of our court hearing, Pietersen waited outside the massive, heavily-guarded police truck. He embraced me tenderly and held my head against his soft, ageing body as he had done on Christmas Day at the Newlands police cells. I clung to him and I remember feeling his tears on my ears. I looked at him sadly wishing to God he was my father and I could take him with me — wherever I was going.

'*My Laaitie*' (my son), said Pietersen sadly, 'don't ever come back to dis *fokken* place; promise Papa Isaak you'll never put your foot in dis jail. Dey gonna kill you for sure.'

I nodded. A baton poked into my backside: 'Move *Boesman; fok* off! The 'government' had the last word.

All eleven of us were discharged. The conflicting evidence of more than ten state witnesses including that of a nine-year-old girl led the Regional Court magistrate to say that he was certain we were killers but there was no tangible evidence with which to convict us. My father had paid for the lawyer.

Back in Sophiatown, the news of our release sparked an all-out vengeance attack by the Headquarters. Many of my gang were badly injured. Seawater, Sesse and Gobee led the attack and challenged me to fight them knife-to-knife. Two months before in the same stinking, lice-infested, urine-dripping police cell, we had broken bread on a Christmas Day. When I looked at my folks who were waiting at my grandpa's house, something in their faces reminded me of a life I'd almost forgotten; almost written off.

But violence, like a shadow, had a way of following me everywhere; to the school which had reluctantly readmitted me and to the church where gang rivals attacked me. The movement of my young, broken and confused life shifted endlessly to and fro; back and forward like motor car gears in the hands of a novice driver. Chops Number Five, the leader of the Headquarters, killed a woman. He was found guilty and jailed for fifteen years but during the first year he died of poisoning.

In May 1957, while I was in standard ten, a son was born to me by a beautiful big-eyed Shangaan girl, Martha. The child meant much to me and I was beginning to look at life a bit differently. There was its mother and her family whom I had grown to love. Things were happening around me that alerted me to new values and a different way of life.

Mrs Mokgosi and her daughter Patricia, both staunch members of the African National Congress, had often asked me to join the movement. I had refused on many occasions but protected them and other women from being molested when they marched through the streets of Sophiatown, Western and Newclare.

The streets no longer appealed to me and some members of my outfit began to question my leadership, especially when I suggested that we disband the Vultures, which had been in the battlefields of Sophiatown since the middle of 1951. I felt a deep unwillingness to fight again, because the streets seemed to have lost their magic, the magnetic force that had drawn me to violence. But how was I to explain my new feeling to the boys I had led up the garden path? How was I to escape when around me my best friends and comrades were being drawn ever deeper into the web of self-destruction? It was a serious tug-of-war between my fervent desire to change my life and my duty to stand up in arms with my brothers. They branded me a coward and one of my closest 'war chiefs', Big Man Senne — in full view of many of our junior members — challenged me to fight him. I refused. He spat in my face and all hell broke loose. Big Man was hospitalised; he had a broken jaw and nose and badly puffed up eyes. I was still the boss, but thrashing Big Man had badly exacerbated our strained relations. The gang split. Most of them teamed up with Big Man and the new outfit was called the Big Man Rush. Word was out that I would be dead before Christmas.

My desire to reform my life was mocked and jeered throughout Sophiatown. But always the wraith of the hanged Pietersen stood before me, reminding me constantly of those hanging jits that waited in the wings to demand and take society's pound of flesh. Fights came like locusts onto the field of my life which I had begun to plough and sow with new and different seeds. I lost some and won some but I decided that genuine rehabilitation would be possible only if I changed friends. Politics became one such friend, but it almost cost me my life.

11. The Change

*M*y metamorphosis from veritable violent beast to human being began in 1955 when the first seeds of political awareness were sown at that historic anti-removals campaign mass meeting. My introduction into the new world, where men and women spoke their minds and openly challenged the police, led me to youth clubs, libraries and education centres. Lectures, debating societies and public meetings took the place of gang hideouts, street corners and dark alleys. Constitutions, preambles and manifestos — strange words to ears accustomed to police whistles and gunshots, war cries and gang calls — replaced guns and knives. And so, a new and exciting world revealed itself to me and a few of my friends who had also grown tired of bloodshed. We took our scars and wounds with us to the debating societies and political education classrooms, took them and held them aloft as trophies earned by our courage. But to our surprise people, especially young folks our age, were not all that impressed by our past and concentrated on educating and refining us in manners and in discipline.

One evening in December of 1956, I attended the usual weekly Western Areas Students' Association political orientation meeting in a study room at the Margaret Holtby Library in Western Native Township. The guest speaker was a trade unionist called Gosane of Alexandra Township, whose son Bob Gosane had made a name as a daring photographer for *Drum* magazine. The previous weekend I had been one of a panel of speakers discussing the need to politicise and assimilate gangsters into the mass movements of the Congress. And who, at the time, was better experienced or qualified to lead the talks than one who had spilled blood; one who was tired of township violence and sought rehabilitation through politics? Old man Gosane was impressed and offered to come to Western Native Township. Ten years later, we were to join hands to fight for the rights of residents there as members of a tenants' association.

After Gosane spoke, Pauline, our chairperson, informed us that Robert Resha was unavailable; he had been arrested the previous day with several other high-ranking officials of the ANC, the Transvaal Indian Congress, the Congress of Democrats and the Textile Workers' Industrial Union. The charge was high treason. The news sparked a flurry of excited discussion among the members, some of who expressed fears of indiscriminate harassment and arrest.

The raids were countrywide and those arrested included lawyers, doctors, professors, schoolteachers and ordinary people. Huge teams of heavily armed special branch policemen conducted midnight and dawn swoops, and many prisoners were flown to Johannesburg to be held at Number Four, whose 'government' had earlier that year placed me under a sentence of death. The raids on political activists began on December 5 after hundreds of arrest warrants had been signed by the chief magistrate of Johannesburg. The high treason charge set the country agog with wagging tongues and the running of frightened feet. Never in the history of this land did the word treason evoke so much debate.

Our history teacher Scheepers, a full blooded Boer nationalist of the Malan and Strijdom stock, suspended ordinary classes to discuss the importance and justification of the treason trial. He told us of the danger of communism which, he asserted, was specifically anti-coloured; anti-anyone of mixed racial origin. We burst out laughing and I asked him if he knew of Robey Leibrandt the Boer fifth-columnist sentenced under the Smuts government to life imprisonment for spying against the Allied Forces. Leibrandt had faced a 'different' kind of high treason charge: at least he was anti-communist, unlike those Congress atheists, said our teacher.

'Your coloured nation will be in peril, the same peril we Boers faced against the hostile Zulus. Support for the communists will alienate you from God,' said Scheepers. Class ended early that day.

Government action had been very swift and our political mentors in the students' association recognised that it would affect the Congress movements. It was trade unionist Lekhotu who said that some back-up or underground infrastructure had to be established in order to thwart the system's destructive machinery.

'We cannot allow Congress to be destroyed through these treason charges. All over the land our leaders are being arrested in the hope that our organisations will die. We must all help to keep the wheels of Congress turning, and hold safe the ideals enshrined in the Freedom Charter. *Mayibuye!*' Lekhotu's thumb shot up and was greeted with the answering cry: '*iAfrika!*'

Among those held were Lionel Morrison, whose cousin Mona was my girlfriend, and Stanley Lollan of the Coloured People's Congress, whose sister Mavis shared the same standard nine class desk with me.

The raids were calculated and thorough. The homes of 150 activists were searched and hundreds of books, newspapers, magazines and political documents were seized to be used as evidence in the treason trial. Perhaps the most shocking arrest at the time was that of the liberal white Member of Parliament for the Western Cape constituency, Mr L B Lee-Warden. Members of our student group were instructed by the ANC's Youth League chapter in Western Native Township to help with fund raising and with the printing and dissemination of anti-government pamphlets. And filled with the zeal and spirit of a young would-be emancipator, I accompanied several students to the ANC office in Fox Street, just off Becker Street opposite the Magistrate's Court complex.

Two reporters, one of them the noted writer Can Themba, were interviewing people there. Words, thousands of them, passed through thin and thick lips with such alacrity that I wondered why there were so many speakers and no listeners. The politicians uttered an avalanche of words, new and old words, exciting and drab; words that evoked a terrible, burning anger in me. Fight, when are we going to fight? Sometimes the looks on the people's faces, their cold frowns, were so palpable they needed no verbal expression.

At the same courts where I had previously appeared on criminal charges, I was amazed at the worldwide interest the treason case had generated in such a short space of time. The public displays of concern and concinnity, the show of force and comradeship among the numerous African, Indian, coloured and white well-wishers and supporters, were in themselves heart-warming. Only at weddings and other social functions had I seen such smartly dressed, sophisticated-looking men and women. Newsmen from the world over mingled with the crowd. When their cameras flashed and clicked, I thought of the Anglican priest called Trevor Huddleston who had sown some of the first seeds of my political awareness. Surely he, who was like a brother to Robert Resha — who in turn was like a friend to street kids and gangsters — would also have been raided by the nocturnal creatures? Surely he too would have stood in the dock beside Luthuli and Mandela, had he not been recalled to England.

Sometimes what we are depends on what we do. . . .

And why were trials where murderers had gruesomely mutilated their victims not given the same publicity? Was the struggle for freedom more important than the loss of human life or the systematic self-destruction of young people in the township streets? I found no answers in the courtroom nor in the eyes of the parties involved in the dangerous tug-of-war drama between the South African government — represented in all instances by the police — and the activists of that day. I watched and absorbed the excitement and din of anxious people, and knew that underneath the jocund frivolity lay tensions and emotions as deep and bitter as those of the man who bit his lip during the arrest of the Indian speaker at the Odin cinema in February of 1955.

When the accused marched into the courtroom from a side door, armed police prevented the people from speaking to them. Luthuli, the broad-shouldered Nelson Mandela and the diminutive Walter Sisulu, whom I had heard at rallies in Newclare and Sophiatown's Freedom Squares, stood motionless and almost impassive; quietly nurturing the flames of an anger that would one day set the country on fire, and jail men for life. The trialists were remanded in custody until December 19 — one year to the day since my own arrest. The total number of those charged with high treason was a staggering 156. That one day in court gave me a glimpse of what the future held for men, women and children who would oppose the apartheid regime. That day in court also taught me that people, especially men, however strong they might appear, were susceptible to pain and suffering.

Sometimes something within us — a sort of hidden strength — collapses and the good that we seek for ourselves and those we love falls apart as well. . . .

We mixed with students and university lecturers, lawyers and doctors, washerwomen and manual labourers; people who said they wanted a share of the fruit of their toil. People who desired only that their children should have a place in the sun, like the children of the white people. Nothing less, nothing more, or so they said. Despite the apparent anger, the heat and vehemence of the protesters, there were times when the appearance of a single police vehicle would send them scampering in all directions.

In September 1957, a public meeting was called on Sophiatown's Freedom Square. Hundreds of people listened attentively with intermittent responses of *'Mayibuye iAfrika!'* as the speakers growled about the removal of their township and the expropriation of their properties.

'An act of violence,' one man said, and shook his head somewhat triumphantly. People would note that he had got up to speak.

'We must protest and agitate and fight back,' another echoed.

'But you will be arrested and beaten up by the police. Your children will suffer. Besides, our numbers are small,' a woman warned the men.

'We have been beaten before; we have suffered long,' one of the men shouted.

There was deafening applause and the meeting got out of hand. The speakers called for order, and one woman started singing an African ditty which warned Verwoerd as it warned Malan and Strijdom that they would be trampled by the car which had no wheels.

The crowd joined in. The singing reached full volume and must have been carried by the wind to the Newlands police, because almost immediately a huge *kwela-kwela* vehicle zoomed along the street. The singing stopped at once.

'*Zinja!*' (Dogs) The leaders and their followers scattered. One woman was arrested, the one who had warned the men about fighting the police. She was bludgeoned and bundled into the vehicle. I watched from an old motor-car where the police could not see me.

It was my final year at school and my fifth month of fatherhood, which took up a lot of time and burdened me with the responsibility of maintaining both son and mother while preparing for the high school graduation examination. My son was one month old when his mother and her family were piled up behind ramshackle furniture and herded into a convoy of army trucks towards the new place called Meadowlands. However exacting and strange the demands of fatherhood were, I was both proud and willing to live up to my new role because it had helped me break the navel cord of the streets. My father, who at first accepted the news of the child uneasily, was pacified by my determination to reform and rehabilitate my confused way of life. He and my grandpa gave me money and gifts for the child whom I named Antonio after my youngest uncle, the last-born child of my grandparents.

On October 9, 1958, one of my favourite henchmen, Maasanto, and Big Man's right-hand man, Benjamin 'Boykie' Ndaba, had an argument over a girl. Boykie demanded a knife duel but I objected and warned him not to go against my decision. He threatened to shoot me and I hit him.

The next morning, Boykie and two others, also former members of the Vultures, waited for me in the alley between Gold and Good Streets. I looked into the muzzle of a revolver I had supplied with bullets, cleaned and kept ready for battle. Deadline, the deserter, called me from behind and as I turned, a bullet burned into my back; another hit an oil barrel that stood near Foy the Chinaman's shop. I dived forward and another bullet grazed my arm. Then, as if by some miracle, two gamblers attacked my would-be assassins with bottles, and they fled into Western. The bullet had entered my sacrum and neatly lodged itself in a permanent resting place. Doctors refused to operate.

Boykie and Deadline paid dearly. Both were tracked down after a two week hunt. Boykie's arms were broken, his stomach ripped open and several gaping wounds and a smashed head were the rewards of his folly. At the time it did not matter to me whether he lived or died. Maasanto helped me to retain my reputation as a force still to be reckoned with and respected.

There were many foul chapters in my troubled and rebellious youth. Chapters of bloodletting, turbulence, misunderstanding and being misunderstood. I lived through them but others in my gang and in rival groups were less fortunate. Some were badly maimed or crippled for life and dozens died violently. Victor, who lived opposite our house, was butchered in broad daylight in the presence of clergymen who had pleaded for his life to be spared. Maasanto's rotting corpse was found in a ditch, badly hacked. Churchill was crushed to death against the wall of his Meadowlands home. Xeko was shot in the mouth by a policeman whom he had stabbed in the back. Former 'war general' of the Vultures, Big Man Jacob Senne, was cut to pieces in a football stadium, but exacted the lives of two of his assailants before he died. Raaphalane and his kid brother Deadline were gunned down, and Boykie who shot me was also Deadline's killer. Boykie went on to kill another co-conspirator in my shooting, a man called States, after both of them had murdered a cinema owner in front of his family. Boykie is in jail now, serving a sentence of 25 years.

Others married and raised families. Two became preachers and many others joined political organisations, like Bennett 'Pantees' Komane, jailed for seventeen years for undergoing military training in Russia and Angola, and returning to South Africa to assist in the overthrow of the regime that would also detain and charge me for my opposition to its system of government; the same regime that was to house-arrest me and restrict my life for eight years, six months and eleven days, after several spells of incarceration incommunicado.

That is another story. . . .

And as I look back sometimes, my heart goes out to my friends and enemies, for while we were destroying others, we destroyed ourselves. But there were other unsung victims in the cruel ghettos; men who laughed in public but cried in private because they had nobody to listen to their lamentations. For if Sophiatown was an intimate and gregarious township of warm and caring citizens, it had its Scrooges and insensitive creatures who like the biblical Pharisee would walk unperturbed over the bodies of the wretched.

Late in 1957, I joined WASA, the Western Areas Student Association, which had its base in Western Native Township. Learned white and black people lectured us on various aspects of life. Dr Ray Phillips spoke on social work. Dr Xuma, formerly the leader of the African National Congress, spoke on health and education and the roles we as youth would be called upon to play. Joe Slovo and a man called Goldberg also addressed our meetings at the home of our WASA colleague Lekhotu, who was a trade unionist and an ANC member. He was banned and house-arrested; his health failed and he died in 1968.

The matchbox house of Lekhotu was filled with young people. I seated myself near an open window; in case of emergency I would be able to make a quick exit. The white men entered and greeted. They shook hands with Lekhotu. Some of us stood up automatically; an old custom, standing up for white people when they entered the room. It was traditional among our fathers and their fathers; and also with us. Nothing new. Customs are strange. . . .

Lekhotu introduced our guests. They were on our side, he said, to help us gain freedom from the whites. It seemed funny though, white against white for the freedom of blacks. The atmosphere became tense and I pinned my eyes on the white men, who said they would be brief as some of us were studying for examinations.

Slovo spoke: 'Comrades and fellow South Africans, I bring you the good wishes of the High Command. We admire your stand in the struggle for freedom. More and more each day, you, your families and friends are being subjected to harsh and unjust measures by the white government.' (How were we to know, I thought. He must mean the police.) He continued: 'You have borne all the hardships with patience and tolerance. But your patience has proven futile against these oppressors. Soon, you are to be told of a master plan that will put an end to all suffering and hardship. Mr Goldberg will later tell you about the new order where there will be no slaves, no masters.' (This was exciting. No masters and no slaves!)

Goldberg rose to speak. Shoulders drooping somewhat, he spoke of communism and socialism, and the need for a system in which all would share equally in the wealth of the land.

He said that it was a pity that Jomo Kenyatta was not in South Africa because men of his calibre had given hope and inspiration to the cause of freedom among all the people of our land. The new order was sweeping the world and Africa. Soon all of the African continent would be free and 'Africa for the Africans' would not be just a slogan, but a reality. Goldberg, a Jew, a white man who spoke about a free Africa; about Kenyatta whom newspapers and white governments had blamed for the killing of hundreds of black people and many whites in Kenya. Here was something new and puzzling, I thought.

It was while Goldberg was speaking that Lekhotu whispered something in his ear. His face changed colour. Slovo bent his head. Both men greeted and told us they would be back. There was no time for questions. Their car sped away through the dusty streets. They had left as suddenly as they had come. A short, shining black man called Mopedi opened a bible and read a few verses about where two and three were gathered in God's name, there was He in their midst. We sang 'God be with you till we meet again'. Two white policemen opened the door and eyed us suspiciously. 'Clever bastards,' said one in Afrikaans. The window near me was wide open.

No masters and no slaves, Goldberg had said. I thought long about his words. Would the new order be different from our system? Were men the property of the state? Would socialism or communism hold the solutions? Would there be an end to prejudice? Should black men, like Jomo Kenyatta, purge the land of all white men, Jews included? And what about the white priest who spoke about love and peaceful change? What about the Ballingers and the Bloombergs? Was none to be spared? And what about my grandfather? Wasn't he a white man? The mystery deepened. With gangsterism it was simple; you knew your enemies and your friends; knives, guns and choppers answered the questions. You had to win or lose; it was easy. But in politics, I discovered, everyone expected to win. The black people had been losing for a long time and now, it appeared, they were tired of losing.

Pamphlets demanding equal pay for equal work were being distributed countrywide. Then came the pound-a-day strike, backed by the ANC. For African workers at the time, a pound a day was a hugely ambitious demand. Meetings were held in Sophiatown, Newclare and Western Native Township. There were brushes between over-enthusiastic police and fiery ANC youth members. People were injured. I was one of them. It was my first encounter with the police outside the usual gang clashes. Their methods were no different, only more determined.

One of the largest crowds gathered at the Newclare Freedom Square to campaign for a minimum wage of one pound a day. Uniformed and special branch police mixed with the crowds. Others sat at a table taking notes of what the speakers said. Top ANC officials and prominent trade union speakers addressed the crowd. Some delegates wore uniforms and others carried the banners of their organisation. The speeches were hot and emotional. They reminded the people of the unjust system of employment and remuneration which robbed them of the basic necessities of life; of good wages for good labour; of owning a share in the economy of the prosperous land; of the need for free education; of rights and the vote; of the vicious pass laws, migrant labour system and influx control that Africans suffered; of the Day of Reckoning, when the wrong would be righted. The response was overwhelming. Shouts of *'Mayibuye iAfrika!'*, and 'Down with white domination!' stirred the passions of the people. I wondered what would have happened if the crowd had had firearms.

The meeting ended peacefully, that is to say without the usual 'incidents' of baton-charging, teargas or crowd retaliation. When the marchers sang, they did so with great gusto and dancing that was delightfully infectious. Young and older men moved with surprising agility, stamping their feet rhythmically and in unison, like African warriors in a war dance. The women, in ANC uniforms or in traditional or western dress, swayed like reeds in the wind. They shook their lithe or buxom bodies and ululated in high-pitched battle-cries — urging on their daring menfolk. Strong, colloquial anthems that seemed to emerge from some hidden recesses of the human spirit touched the windows, the doors and the rooftops with a bewitching, magnetic strain that reached into the heart. The fascinated and the curious, the brave and the fearful, children and adults, joined the ever-swelling ranks of the marchers from Newclare through Western Native Township and into Sophiatown.

Singing. The kind that comes before conquest and triumph. Songs of daring and commitment before the final attack; singing, as only the African sings in the face of great adversity.

When the crowd marched into Sophiatown's Good Street, I broke away to join some of my friends at Goldberg's chemist in Main Road which divided the two townships. A coloured watch repairer, Boeta Michaels, and his family were pushing their car from Main Road into our street where they lived. A black policeman ordered them to leave the car on the side of the road. An argument ensued and Boeta Michaels was felled by a baton blow. I attacked and beat the policeman to the ground. Several of his colleagues appeared and tried to arrest me. But members of my gang came to my rescue and — to the delight of many bystanders — we chased the policemen down the road. People suddenly scattered as four heavily-armed Boer policemen jumped out of a squad car and began shooting in the air. One called Vyver bashed me in the face. I came to in the yard of the Newlands police station, handcuffed to the wire fence. Blood blurred my vision, and my mouth was thick and dry with the gore. I could not even speak properly.

'He is one of those pound-a-day people,' lied the black policeman I had assaulted. Suddenly I felt two hard, crushing blows in my ribcage. My shins were vengefully kicked and my throat was in terrible pain from all the choking. My father arrived and pleaded for my release. The steel bangles were removed and I slumped into his strong arms. Safe, God; safe at last. . . .

My face was a ghastly sight. My eyes were all puffed and swollen, my lips felt like sausages and my throat was scratched and blue. The police accompanied my father and me to hospital and told the doctor I had been beaten by a crowd of rioting natives, and they had rescued me. My father did not say a word and I therefore assumed he'd made a deal with them. Vyver told him to bring me to the station to lay charges. It was a joke, it must have been, because I saw my father laugh. I guess I would have laughed as well but for the pain.

One of the many strikes and boycotts we supported in Sophiatown concerned the deplorable working and living conditions at prison farms and labour camps. A team of black journalists discovered a prisoner's skull in a potato field. It was alleged that he had been murdered and buried by a white farmer. The ANC called for a boycott of potatoes, the impact of which was devastating. The State was pressed by liberals and religious institutions for an inquiry into the farm labour system, with emphasis on better pay and improved working conditions. Millions of potatoes rotted on the farms and in markets, in shops and on hawkers' lorries. The people meant business.

Then came the protest by African women against legislation forcing them to carry passes like their menfolk. Lilian Ngoyi, the woman who had wept when Nkosi Sikelele was sung in the Odin cinema, led the women through the township streets. Women everywhere were protesting and singing. The police were accused of beating the women. Several policemen were attacked and injured and the protesters arrested and finally suppressed.

. . .Was it not enough that their husbands, brothers, sons and fathers were already humiliated by the pass laws? Not enough that their menfolk were hounded like murderers for the document of their existence? Not enough that the men had to strip naked and stand at the Pass Office, while a white 'doctor' hit at their penises and buttocks to certify them healthy. These women's fathers, sons and husbands had been reduced to half-humans. Now it would be their turn.

Most of the strikes, boycotts and other anti-government incidents preceded or coincided with the removal of Sophiatown. Elated by the success of the bus boycotts and the potato boycott, the ANC anticipated greater victories because the people were directly involved. Through the removals, the ANC and its many allies gambled on an uprising which would spark national insurrection and eventually result in the overthrow of the Nationalist Government.

12. The Big Move

*E*xcitement ran high as meetings were held on township squares, street-corners and in churches. The people were urged not to move and the ANC promised to stand by them. Most stand-owners and businessmen exploited the political platforms for their own gain because the removals would mean a decline in profits and finally, loss of livelihood. But not all the people were businessmen and property owners. Some lived in horrible conditions and the promise of four-roomed houses doused the spirit of revolution in many of them. There were mixed feelings. However, the agitation increased, followed always by the usual police harassment. Houses, shops and church-walls were painted in bold letters with defiant graffiti:

WE WILL NOT MOVE. WE WOULD RATHER DIE!

HE WHO COMES TO DESTROY WILL HIMSELF BE DESTROYED!
FREEDOM FOR OUR CHILDREN!

Bands of young people marched through the streets of Sophiatown and Newclare, carrying posters. Many were arrested, among them students and journalists; they paid admission of guilt fines and returned to the streets to protest and march again. Foreign newsmen and local journalists virtually lived in Sophiatown. They wanted to see it all; see the revolution in its initial stages. It was coming for sure, so we all believed.

For many of the homeless and destitute the removals augured well, for the sly government protagonists advised them to move. Were they not going to get their own houses with a large yard for their children to play in, and their own taps and lavatories? Was that not what they wanted? They would be away from the leeching Indian, Chinese and white businessmen; away from the unproductive coloureds. There would be businesses and money and even power. Did not the big *baas* Verwoerd promise all this.

And so, the people sang. . . .

. . . Are we not leaving behind the rusty tin shacks and crowded hovels? Nights of terror and uncertainty? Nights of death? Perhaps in the new place called Meadowlands it will be different. Perhaps our sons will become men before being cut down by violence and gangsterism. Perhaps our daughters will not become mothers before their time. Perhaps we will make love without the children peeping and laughing through the curtains dividing the room. Perhaps there will be peace of mind and escape from the cruel hands of the police. Perhaps, perhaps, Lord, perhaps. . . .

On a dark morning early in the winter of 1955, a strong contingent of police, soldiers and saracen tanks surrounded Sophiatown. The armed units stood on alert as army trucks moved into the silent streets. There had been talk and promises by the ANC of resistance and revolt. The sun rose and briefly touched the shacks and houses.

A child must have stirred.

And dawn came. But it would be a day different from all other days. The beginning of the end. Rain, slow and deliberate, pattered down on the town. Too moved, perhaps too cowardly, the sun hid its face behind grey clouds. Bewilderment, laughter and strange expectation showed on the dark faces. Then, the move began, slow and deliberate like the rain.

In Bertha Street, I saw Father Huddleston help one family. A tall government employee who was directing the removals spat as the priest turned around. I cannot say that he spat at the priest, only that he did spit. I took in every detail of the move that my eyes could see. The wind lashed the people's faces and the heavy-coated soldiers and the black policemen carried furniture to the waiting trucks. The priest smiled now and then, but his smiles gave no warmth. Perhaps it was the waving and calling, the tears of mixed feelings. Excitement and expectancy. And laughter and disappointment. Some people were singing: 'Let's leave, O my children, let's leave Sophia alone, let's go to a place where we'll stay in peace, let's go to Meadowlands.'

A group of student protesters marched down Bertha Street. They were surrounded and quickly hustled into a police van. Journalists from the world over had come for the revolt. They were disappointed, as lorries rode westward free of incident. A smile of victory must have crossed the face of Dr Verwoerd wherever he was.

The exodus to Meadowlands was a long and tedious affair. The authorities must have wondered where all the people came from, because the more they moved, the more people there seemed to be. Shrewd politicians and businessmen who owned properties induced rural Africans to inhabit the vacant houses. The numbers swelled until the government authorities and the police introduced a permit system. When Klopper the Vicious stepped in, the night raids resulted in mass arrests. Bribery and corruption usually followed because the people always offered money. Those who could not pay were jailed. Men, women and children became the victims of the government's brutal campaign to discourage unregistered tenants as well as the remnants of the won't-moves. I have vivid recollections of those raids, when families scurried like squirrels and slept in the open veld and the broken-down buildings. Some took refuge in our yard. We were coloured and thus temporarily immune to this one form of hardship. But it was inevitable that we too, would be forced to sell and move. It was just a matter of time.

In August of 1954 — nine months prior to the first removals, various individuals; churchmen, politicians to the left, social workers and political scientists, local and foreign — had warned the Prime Minister, Dr Hendrik Verwoerd, that his decision to resettle the urban Africans of Johannesburg's western areas on an ethnic basis would result in faction warfare. Spokesmen from white liberal-orientated organisations also expressed grave misgivings about the enforcement of tribal apartheid on Africans who had lived in cosmopolitan townships such as Vrededorp, Alexandra Township and Sophiatown. Certain Native Advisory Board officials — known at the time for their docility regarding politically contentious matters — publicly opposed Verwoerd's proposals, which they said would only exacerbate the tensions already created by the government's decision to remove the Africans at gunpoint if need be. The white anti-government groups said Verwoerd's plan would further frustrate relations between the state and the African people, who saw the policy as another divide-and-rule tactic.

But Verwoerd was determined to rewrite history and show the world and South Africa that the Boers were not only masters of their own destinies, but also the captains of black people's souls.

Meadowlands and Diepkloof, which were to accommodate the African people evicted from the cosmopolitan townships, were accordingly divided into tribal sub-sections, the Nguni language groups, with the Shangaans and Vendas, carefully separated from the Sothos and Tswanas. The single-sex hostels for migrant workers, in these areas and in Dube, housed mostly Zulus.

Verwoerd had told South Africa and the world that ethnic separation would not cause any violence. But in early September of 1957, bloody battles began in Meadowlands and Dube and several other south-western townships of Johannesburg. Hundreds of Zulus and Basothos fought each other savagely with an assortment of weapons, ranging from guns to home-made swords. Forty men died among whom were five Zulu warriors shot dead by police using sten-guns. More than a hundred Africans were admitted to hospitals, and some of them later died of their wounds.

The odour of death pervaded the township of Meadowlands as strong units of police cordoned off the danger spots only after much damage. Bloodstained weapons were scattered on the dusty township streets and cries of protest and fear echoed in the halls, the churches and the corridors of the white Parliament, but Verwoerd would not relent.

The tribal wars spread to the single-sex hostels in the city of Johannesburg and outlying Reef areas, increasing the death toll as well as the number of injured and maimed. The government's policy of enforced tribal grouping was roundly condemned and blamed as the primary cause of the inter-tribal slaughtering. The rage of unrest — which the police had guaranteed the frightened white voters would not come to the city — sparked off at several mines. Police gunfire and baton-charges were the order of the day. The death toll rose as fierce violence continued. The Basotho clan — known as 'Russians' or 'Ma-Russia' lost several top men. Zulu faction leaders claimed the police had sided with the Russians — and some people in the city laughed at the paradox — the South African Police in league with Russians — while death continued to ravage the townships.

But the stubborn and arrogant Verwoerd blamed the *tsotsi* element and sternly warned that 'hooligans' would be deported to their 'home' territories, whatever that meant.

A newspaper editorial in *The Star* of 16 September 1957 ran: 'The brutal and bloody clashes between Zulu and Basotho factions in the townships indicate both a residual savagery among many Native people of our urban communities and a failure of the European civilisation mission. . . . ' *The Star* was an opposition paper!

Crime reporters wrote that Mau-Mau tactics were being used in the clashes. The police were praised for their firm action in quelling the unrest.

The white local authority councillors blamed the government's ethnic grouping policy. But the shrewd Dr Verwoerd blamed the local authorities for lack of control over their so-called '*tsotsi* element'. Government supporting whites believed Verwoerd's analysis. And while the whites blamed each other, scores of Africans were butchered to death.

More than three thousand policemen and soldiers were put on alert as the clashes continued. African homes were raided for weapons and 'unemployed hooligans'. The white policemen were armed with automatic guns and rifles and their black colleagues carried spears. The raids were apparently effective for by late September of 1957, all was quiet — for a while. The peace pow wows arranged by 'concerned' whites and frightened black leaders came to nothing because leaders of warring factions, especially the Zulus, refused to attend the meetings.

The local authority instituted its own commission of inquiry in view of the government's refusal to probe the tribal violence. Three retired judges, A. van der Sandt Centlivres, E.R. Roper and L. Greenberg agreed to head the commission.

High on the list of those who blamed the government for the clashes was the then Anglican Bishop of Johannesburg, Bishop Ambrose Reeves. He said — and many thousands of blacks and some whites shared his views — 'There were far deeper causes for the riots in Dube and Meadowlands. . . .' Bishop Reeves cited lack of communication and failure on the part of the white people to give the Africans a greater say in their own affairs. Most of all, he blamed Verwoerd's government and called for an end to ethnic grouping.

The ANC's Oliver Tambo submitted a memorandum to the commission of inquiry, also blaming the state and bitterly condemning the 'brutal behaviour' of the South African Police, whom he and countless other individuals and organisations accused of 'mishandling, assaulting and insulting township folk. . . . Miserable wages, ethnic grouping, the general apartheid policy and the continual hounding of the African people are only some of the causes,' said the ANC document.

When the three judges submitted their reports, it was found that four-fifths of the African people who resided in the resettled areas in south-western townships of Johannesburg (later to become Soweto) lived on or below the poverty line. Other findings were:

★ A complete breakdown of parental authority in most cases.
★ Abundant evidence that the police had been unable to cope with the gangs that infest the townships.
★ Tribal grouping was a direct cause of the township riots.

It was clear to the commissioners that any sectional grouping, whether in housing, schools, sports clubs, or anywhere else, was likely to produce sectional feelings 'which comparatively primitive and uncivilised people are prone to develop into dangerous antagonisms and concerted displays of violence. . . .'

Dr Verwoerd laughed at the findings and dismissed them as exaggerations inspired by liberals.

We were among the last coloured families to be removed. The township was ravaged by demolition squads and only a few buildings, shops and the Christ The King Anglican Church remained. After the demolition of houses young boys looked for valuables under the flooring of the shacks. Others collected copper and brass. Men and women cleaned bricks which they sold to building contractors. There was money in destruction. And there was longing. I often stood on the verandah of my grandfather's house and strained my ears for familiar noises like the bright, sharp whistling of the milkman, the sound of milk bottles kissing each other as they parted ways. Many of my friends and enemies had gone. The two cinemas — Odin and Balanski — previously the scenes of heavy gang clashes and political rallies, were quiet and subdued.

Dan Siwisa, the ANC man who had said 'Africa is not dying,' had himself died in detention — from natural causes it was found. Several politicians known to me were arrested for treason against the State. The two political lecturers, Comrades Slovo and Goldberg, were among them. They had been released and the newspapers reported several persons self-exiled. Others were banned or re-arrested. Lekhotu was among them. My father feared that I would be arrested for my part in the assault on the police during the clashes in 1958 in Sophiatown and Newclare, and wanted to send me away, but I refused.

Something was dying inside of me; small and unnoticeable, but dying nonetheless. Perhaps it had something to do with the change and decay around me. Or the sweet memories that had gone with the twilight.

Our departure from the old houses at 16 Gerty Street was sad because our once closely-knit family was scattered without hope of reunion. It seemed that by moving out of our houses, we had in fact volunteered our final destruction. It may be thought melodramatic, but I swear that when I walked out of my grandpa's house, I heard the soft, deep voice of my granny, untroubled and reassuring, emerging from the mist and clutch of the grave. Her voice rekindled my joy and lifted my spirits. Home was where I wanted to be, wanted to remain until the end of my days.

Outside in the yard, my grandpa's ancient sideboard and its extraordinarily long dinner table with fourteen chairs were gently loaded onto a truck. The vintage radio and Victorian-style brass bed took with them the odour of furniture and family that could warm any death-house. Everything was finally loaded and I jumped on. My grandpa moved slowly around the massive yard like a storeman performing the annual stock-taking. But for my Papa-mio there would not be a replenishing of the dwindling stocks; no return to the houses that he as an immigrant Italian miner had built for his coloured family and its offspring. And as I looked at him a strength beyond me and emanating from filial fondness flowed through my veins and revitalised my being with a determination to survive the destruction, because the house was only part of the whole. What was inside of us, our dignity and our humanity as a generous, compassionate and charitable family, was beyond the reach of the crushing bulldozers or the might of the system.

My father and his new wife — three years my junior, and the mother of a son — moved to Bosmont township, built specifically to house coloured families evicted from Albertsville, Sophiatown and the 'white suburb' of Newlands. My four uncles, their 'wives' and children; my aunt Baby and her family — which included her only son Chossie, his wife Sybil and their two daughters — took the dingy two-room shacks vacated by Africans in Western Native Township. Gone were the pomp and affluence of the olden days. There wasn't much money left in my grandpa's coffers as most of his wealth had been shared between his children. A shrewd Italian lawyer had absconded to Italy with several thousand pounds my grandpa had given him to hold in trust. The buses had also been sold, and his shares in an Italian food company, so that there was no income at all. The 'princes' and 'princesses' of the Mattera clan were forced into a lifestyle of synthetic 'colouredness'; like the debris and dirt that the government bulldozers were piling into huge rubble-heaps. But I refused to be part of the debris. I knew that what I was and would someday become had sprung from a different and better source. What did it mean to be 'coloured'? And would our becoming 'coloured' nullify the gregariousness that Sophiatown had woven into the fabric of our family? We had been called *bruin mense* (brown people) with stronger ties to white — and whatever 'black blood' pumped though our veins would diminish with the passage of time. So said Dr Verwoerd, and many coloureds believed him.

And as if it were some Nemesis for him, my grandfather was spared to witness the burials of four of his children: Aunt Baby and my uncles Willie, Danny and Goon, and some of his grandchildren, in quick succession. He was spared to witness the destruction of Sophiatown and its unique way of life, and above all, he was spared to watch his kingdom fall. When the house he rented in Albertsville was also demolished, the authorities allowed him to live with his eldest daughter in Bosmont under a five-year permit. He did not live to have the permit renewed. Although he used to laugh a great deal while he related stories about his youth in Italy or about the many fights he had with Afrikaner miners over his fondness for Africans, my grandpa's eyes often revealed an inexpressible agony. It was over something we could not weigh or determine. For how can pain be measured, when there are some scales that the human eye cannot perceive?

An alien in an alien land was my grandfather's official statistic; never belonging and never being part of the South African experience. Only that segment of it called coloured which he had sought and created from the loins of a woman of Xhosa and Khoisan origins. When my grandmother took her white 'Taliaana' lover to her parents at Graaff Reinet in the Cape Province, she was seventeen years old and deeply in love. Her father, a tall Xhosa named Rawana (pronounced Gaawana) was a sheep shearer and herder who owned a small plot of land on which he had built a large mud and plank house for his yellow-skinned Khoisan wife and their four children. Above their simple house towered the imposing mountains of 'Gaaf' as the local Graaff Reinetans called their village, 'the gem of the Karoo'. The young sailor could not communicate with his prospective in-laws and sat motionless and almost impassive as his betrothed explained to her family that she loved the foreigner, whose language she would learn. And what of the traditional *lobola*, the payment her Taliaana, like any other suitor, must make to her father, to secure the right to give his name to his bride and his offspring? And what of the young girl who must, according to the custom, spread out the mat for the negotiation? For was not she, U-Minnie Thandeka (the loved one), the eldest of Rawana's flock, the first fruit and mirror of his own marriage? The *lobola* would follow as all things did to them that waited. . . .

It was Rawana'a widow who received the money.

Rawana did not live to see the children that would come from his daughter's womb; children with fair skins and cold, grey-blue eyes, children who would learn the language of their Neapolitan father and master most of the indigenous languages of the African people. Rawana's wife, who had heavy locks of hair, and of whom I have fond memories, left Graaff Reinet to live and die in my grandfather's Sophiatown house. In his broken English, my grandpa would recall his days in Graaff Reinet in the mud house near the foot of the mountains, where the proud Xhosa herder had asked for his *lobola*. The woman he then married in a Dutch Reformed church gave him eight children — five of whom he buried.

On the evening of his death at my aunt's Bosmont home, my Papa-mio was in jocund spirits. Songs of his native Italy, made famous by Caruso and Beniamino Gigli, rang through the house. We were taken aback by the vibrant quality of his voice as he strutted around the house, into his room and then into the yard. He sang 'Santa Lucia' so loudly, the dogs barked as they would at a drunk. I thought he was going to burst a vein or snap his vocal cords.

'Papa, is late; you cumma inside,' I said, copying his manner of speaking.

But the old man ignored me, and strutted around the house. I noticed that he was without his walking stick. He walked up to me, arms outstretched, and embraced and kissed me in the traditional Italian fashion as if I were a friend or relation he had not seen in many years. He then hummed his way into his room and locked the door.

'Tatson!' he shouted from his room. 'Tomorra you buya cigara; me giva you money.' I replied yes, and walked home to Western Native Township. I could not guess that he was going to die the next day. I woke up with the perpetual hope of seeing a better day; of giving a word of encouragement to my folks in Western who daily complained of hardships. Somehow I could not get things done and only arrived at my aunt's house towards sunset.

He was dead.

His favourite brightly coloured scarf was still neatly tied around his neck. He had put on his best three-piece 'bird's eye' suit, complete with the solid gold watch and chain.

'He packed all his clothes and told me he was going home; home to his people and his country,' said my aunt without a note of sadness in her voice. She said she had been puzzled by his high spirits and happy mood. He had sat in his rocking chair of many, many years, and hummed softly until the rocking ceased.

And so, another vital fragment of the dream was laid to rest in a cemetery designated by law for black people only. He lies just a stone's throw from his children and about 200 yards from his bride from Graaff Reinet.

'You no putta stone on my grave,' he once said to my father. But for an old African beer pot, his grave lies unmarked.

Life took a new and strange turn. Coloureds from all the condemned and affected areas in and around the city of Johannesburg were dumped in Western. Whole families and once stable communities were forcibly uprooted along with the Indians, who were resettled about thirty miles from Johannesburg. The Africans had been first in the long queue for destruction and displacement. It was the turn of the coloureds, and their arrival brought new uncertainties and new strife to Western. The people spoke a language foreign to my soul, filled with those hostilities that arise only from insecurity and fear and misunderstanding. Some coloureds, ironically the dark-skinned ones (perhaps out of fear of contamination), spoke derogatorily about 'kaffirs' and 'coolies'. My values and norms, the very essence of my existence as a product of a cosmopolitan lifestyle and code of conduct, were ridiculed and challenged. People were afraid to speak African languages or tune their radios to a black station. Association would mean a common identity with all the humiliation, debasement and suffering that the African experienced.

. . . Oh great God; anything but that. Oh *wit baas* call me *Hotnot, Boesman, Geelbek* (Yellow-mouth); anything but native, kaffir! *Baas* spare me that insult, though I am blacker than the Ace of Spades. . . .

'Call me anything, my *baas*. . . .'

Their words evoked a strange anger in me. I could not comprehend their rejection of being African, which I myself had tried so hard to be despite the fact that I did not suffer the same humiliation, hardships and scorn as did the African people. Here was something new and perplexing. People whose skins were as black as tar, whose hair was as short and woolly as that of the Africans, were saying to the white man: '*Baas*, call me by any other insulting name but native or kaffir. . . .'

. . . Ah, the people who are neither black nor white but live a twilight existence — half free, half slaves to the laws and whims of apartheid. . . .

They poured into Western, a boiling cauldron of fear and suspicion, of despair and degradation such as only the Group Areas Act can cause. I listened to the pounding heart-beat of these twilight people, and to the laughter and crying that burst from their mouths like vomit, and I knew that deep inside I would always be a stranger among them. Not that I was aloof or indifferent to their pain, but I could not see myself accepting the status of a twilight person. More than anything else in the world, I wanted to act and be accepted as an African.

Life changed dramatically.

Western became terribly overpopulated with this new creation — each person trying hard to outwit and, to coin a word, 'out-coloured' the other in mannerisms and speech in their emulation of whiteness. Shebeens mushroomed throughout the township and a wave of violence, immorality and squalor swept over us. Radios roared full blast. The noise was unbearable, reaching its peak at weekends. Music that burst and rose in a crescendo of insanity. Loud. Sickening.

Western on the prowl.

Fridays — derogatorily called '*Boesmans* Christmas' by all and sundry, black and white — was the worst day of the week. And I could not understand why that noise, that terrible weeping and bitter-sweet agony — a sort of supplication — could not reach the ears of God. Here was His creation, into which I had been classified, lost and bewildered and misplaced among men. A twilight people who although born of blood and flesh and spirit — like the rest of mankind in South Africa — were being conceived on the drawing board of apartheid. A hybrid species, signed, sealed and stamped into synthetic nationhood.

It comes to me in the night. Those cries, those laughing people who come from wherever they came from, and brought with them an unyielding noise that permeated the night air and sank into a deep hole in my body. Sophiatown in all her gory and gruesome days of blood and death seemed to vanish into insignificance for me. I could not endure Western. Each street became a slum of its own as men, women and children rubbed against each other the same slime and frustration they had picked up from others.

Liquor and loose women.

Money and lustful men.

People fighting.

People dying.

Neither black nor white; living and dying in a twilight world created by the white man, the Christian whose Covenant it was to lead the coloureds to nationhood and race pride.

They were leading us to hell.

And beyond the iron railing that surrounded the prison called Western Coloured Township, beyond the tramline and across the legendary Main Road, scene of intense gang rivalry and escapades of juvenile delinquency, stood the high rubble of smashed bricks and debris. Beneath it lay Kofifi-Sophia, unable to give a hint of life, of defiance. She was buried deep under the weight and power of the tin gods whose bulldozers, like the terrible bombs of war, had razed our homes, our hopes and dreams, and what little love and comfort and peace Sophiatown had given us.

Gone.

Buried.

Covered by the dust of defeat — or so the conquerors believed. But there is nothing that can be hidden from the mind. Nothing that memory cannot reach or touch or call back.

Memory is a weapon.

I knew deep down inside of me, in that place where laws and guns cannot reach nor jackboots trample, that there had been no defeat. In another day, another time, we would emerge to reclaim our dignity and our land. It was only a matter of time and Sophiatown would be reborn.

The world became alien and I felt lost.

About the Author

Don Mattera was born in Sophiatown in 1935, but his family origins in South Africa go back to 1904 when his grandfather, Francesco, a sailor from Naples, jumped ship in Cape Town and married a black South African woman. Though socially unacceptable, mixed marriage was then legally permissible in South Africa. After working in the Kimberley diamond mines, Francesco moved to Sophiatown in the late 1920s where he established a bus company for African commuters. Don Mattera was largely raised by his paternal grandparents who sent him to a private Catholic convent where he became proficient in English and boxing. In his teenage years he rebelled against his strict upbringing and joined the Vultures, a notorious streetland gang whose leadership he quickly assumed.

For seven years the gang terrorized Sophiatown; most of its members died violently and Mattera himself narrowly survived three shoot-outs. Acquitted of murder in the mid-1950s, he served several short sentences for public violence. By then Sophiatown's resistance to its demolition was growing and Mattera threw his considerable talents into that campaign. Politicized by the experience, he joined the ANC Youth League.

In the early 1970s Mattera became active in black consciousness politics and, as a reporter, helped found the Union of Black Journalists. In 1973 he was banned and house-arrested, a condition he endured for eight and a half years. In an "Open Letter" to white South Africans, he described his life as a banned person: "I am and I am not. I am dead and yet at the same time I live." After his banning order was lifted, he resumed political activity as an executive member of the National Forum, became a director of Skotaville, a new black consciousness publisher, and wrote the widely acclaimed poetry collection, *Azanian Love Song* (1983).

Don Mattera is also a dramatist. His published plays include *One Time, Brother* (banned in 1984) and *Kagiso Sechaba*. Among the literary prizes he has won are the African Writers Citation (African Writers Association, 1979); the Kwanzaa Award (given in New York to him and five other South African authors); the Steve Biko Prize (Stockholm, 1986) and the Kurt Tucholsky Award (World PEN Association, 1986). In 1986 he helped found the Congress of South African Writers.